D1559598

Pilgrimage to Puritanism

Studies in Church History

William L. Fox
General Editor

Vol. 9

PETER LANG
New York • Washington, D.C./Baltimore • Boston
Bern • Frankfurt am Main • Berlin • Vienna • Paris

Dan G. Danner

Pilgrimage to Puritanism

History and Theology
of the Marian Exiles
at Geneva, 1555–1560

PETER LANG
New York • Washington, D.C./Baltimore • Boston
Bern • Frankfurt am Main • Berlin • Vienna • Paris

Library of Congress Cataloging-in-Publication Data

Danner, Dan G.
Pilgrimage to Puritanism: history and theology
of the Marian exiles at Geneva, 1555–1560 / Dan G. Danner.
p. cm. — (Studies in church history; v. 9)
Includes bibliographical references and index.
1. Refugees, Religious—England—History—16th century. 2. Refugees, Religious—
Switzerland—Geneva—History—16th century. 3. Church
of England—Doctrines—History—16th century. 4. Reformed Church—
Switzerland—Geneva—Doctrines—History—16th century. 5. England—Church
history—16th century. 6. Geneva (Switzerland)—Church history—16th century.
7. Puritans—England—History—16th century. I. Title.
II. Series: Studies in church history (New York, N.Y.); vol. 9.
BR377.D36   272'.6—dc21   97-26602
ISBN 0-8204-3884-7
ISSN 1074-6749

Die Deutsche Bibliothek-CIP-Einheitsaufnahme

Danner, Dan G.:
Pilgrimage to puritanism: history and theology of the Marian exiles at Geneva,
1555–1560 / Dan G. Danner. –New York; Washington, D.C./Baltimore;
Boston; Bern; Frankfurt am Main; Berlin; Vienna; Paris: Lang.
(Studies in church history; Vol. 9)
ISBN 0-8204-3884-7

Cover design by James F. Brisson.

The paper in this book meets the guidelines for permanence and durability
of the Committee on Production Guidelines for Book Longevity
of the Council of Library Resources.

Printed in the United States of America.

To Dorothy

ACKNOWLEDGMENTS

The author would like to acknowledge the assistance of the Folger Shakespeare Library and the University of Portland for fellowships and research grants which helped to bring this project to fruition. In addition, the staffs of the British Museum, Cambridge University Library, the Bodlein Library, the National Library of Scotland, and the Henry Huntington Library were extremely helpful in getting me to sources necessary to do research.

On a more personal level, James C. Spalding of the School of Religion at the University of Iowa has been a helpful and inspirational mentor for many years; indeed, it was he who first titillated my interest in the English Reformation and puritan theology.

I would like to thank James D. Moore, Professor of Political Science at the University of Portland, for his expertise and understanding in helping me prepare the manuscript.

Special acknowledgment is also due my family. My spouse, Dorothy Holland Danner and sons J Darin and Kirt always seemed to exhibit the right kind of patience and support. There have been many hands and minds which have contributed to the realization of this project, and they must accept my gratitude anonymously. No one, obviously, must bare the blame for whatever shortcomings the book might have except its author, but many souls may share whatever plaudits might come its way.

TABLE OF CONTENTS

INTRODUCTION

THE GENEVA EXILES AND RECENT ENGLISH REFORMATION HISTORIOGRAPHY

E nglish Reformation studies have undergone significant revision since the work of A. F. Pollard during the first half of the twentieth century. Pollard contended in several works[1] that the primary task in understanding the Reformation in England was to uncover the legacy of Henry VIII. Pollard believed that the people of England gave Henry freedom to pursue his policies which entailed not so much a doctrinal reform but "an episode in the eternal dispute between Church and State."[2] The cause of the Reformation was not Henry's divorce but the King's determination to be supreme in England; the divorce thus became politically expedient for the King's need to have a legitimate male heir. As Henry realized that his interests coincided with those of the middle classes, he championed parliamentary privileges and constitutional law. As a chapter in the history of the rising nationalism of the sixteenth century, the English Reformation was thus not a spontaneous revolution by clergy against Rome or even a genuine reformation of church doctrine.

This interpretation was challenged after World War II by G. R. Elton.[3] Elton's empirical approach depicted Henry VIII as fairly un-interested in the day-to-day business of the monarchy which allowed Thomas Cromwell the opportunity to implement his own version of reform, part of the process of which included certain changes in reli-gion and the church. The person most responsible for the Reformation in England was Cromwell, not Henry, and the divorce as well as the reformation in religion was a political act and not an ex-pression of Cromwell's dislike for Catholicism. The break with Rome became the essence of the English Reformation as a consequence.[4] Elton's interpretation has been challenged by Joel Hurstfield[5] and J. J. Scarisbrick.[6]

The noted English religious historian, A. G. Dickens, views Henry and Cromwell from a different perspective. As a student of the

Continental Reformation and late medieval religion, Dickens was convinced that the Reformation in England took place within the context of the erosion of an older, Catholic church which by the 1530s had given way to a Protestantism gaining momentum that Henry could not stop. The breach with Rome became the last straw orchestrated by the creative and opportunistic Cromwell. Thus while Elton focused on the political scene (and religion as only one component within the matrix) Dickens highlighted in great detail the religious scene, the only modern English historian to emphasize the importance of the specifically religious and theological components of the English Reformation.[7]

Since the 1960s, however, English Reformation historiography has gotten more complex and the debate over interpretation more intense. The religious component usually co-opted by historical theologians and intellectual historians must now share ground in a larger, interdisciplinary context where sociological, psychological and economic issues are equally paramount; indeed, one can see the ghosts of Marx, Freud and Weber behind the scenes in much recent English Reformation historiography.

The debate over the causes of the Reformation continues. Elton views the religious component within the context of a political movement and concludes that the Reformation came "from above" via coercion. He is joined by those whose views of Henry VIII are arguably different from his such as Scarisbrick and Christopher Haigh. Haigh has introduced another component into the admixture by raising the issue of the pace of change of the Reformation in England. Both he and Scarisbrick lead a school of interpretation which departs from Dickens' contention of a fairly fast-paced reformation with early inroads of Protestantism, and concludes that reformation really did not happen in any intrinsic sense until the time of Elizabeth.[8] So the Scarisbrick-Haigh interpretation of the Reformation in England is that it was indeed imposed by the government upon the people of England, that the ordinary person in the countryside was not unhappy with medieval Catholicism at all, and that the Reformation was an unwelcome event which dragged along without popular impetus until well into the reign of Elizabeth. Christopher Haigh's important study of Lancashire[9] was the impetus for this interpretation.

The Scarisbrick-Haigh interpretation dismisses the influence of the Lollards, the Cambridge Lutherans who gathered at the White Horse Inn in Cambridge, and a general feeling of anti-clericalism that Dickens and his school views as important. Dickens is the scholar who seems to have taken the most care in studying Lollardy and the late medieval religious milieu in England. He is convinced that Lollardy had a wider appeal than the *devotio moderna* in England, and that it merged in some localities with the interest in the Bible in the vernacular of which Tyndale's New Testament was the primary example. Lollardy precluded a Catholic reform by hardening the minds of English bishops and their officials into a sterile, negative and rigid attitude towards all criticism and towards the scriptures in English. Thus the groundwork had been prepared for the critical dissent necessary for the Protestant Reformation.[10] Haigh's study of Lancashire, however, indicated that there was little if any Lollard sentiment in this countryside, that anti-clericalism was almost non-existent, and that Roman Catholicism was doing fine in England until trade and commercial routes were opened up to London and the southern towns which allowed academically trained theologians and preachers to come in and create havoc. Thus the Reformation was not an indigenous movement from the grass-roots of dissent and anti-clericalism but an unwelcome and unsuspecting imported product.[11]

Thus the terrain aspect of the debate centers on whether the Reformation came "from above" by the imposition of the monarchy, or "from below" through the waning of medieval Catholicism exemplified in such movements as Lollardy, a general anti-clericalism characteristic of a wider European reformation, and Christian humanism which sought reforms through education and learning. In addition, the pace aspect of the debate juxtaposes foci from a slow, plodding and unwelcome process to one which came fairly quickly and prepared England for the kind of event similar in nature to Continental reforms in Wittenberg, Zurich and Geneva. The pace aspect of the debate also gives historians the opportunity to posit Henry's own religious persuasion, and again the spectrum expands from the view that had Henry's reign lasted a while longer he would have become himself a Protestant[12] to the view that he remained Catholic to his death—he simply was no papist.[13] Which side of the spectrum one finds convincing also determines why and how far Henry entrusted the education of his son to would-be Protestants.[14]

The emphasis in much of recent English Reformation historiography has been the study of wills and the attempt to engage in local studies, and much of this effort can be traced to the sharp edges of the debate between the Dickens paradigm and the Haigh paradigm. The resolution is to quantify matters, to "count heads" in order to see whose paradigm can stand the test of the evidence. Yet, how does one measure the success of Protestantism or the failure of Catholicism, the vitality of the existing spiritual foundations and the resistance to newfangled popular forms of religiosity? How can church attendance actually be quantifiable? Do wills and their preambles actually reveal

religious affiliations, indeed affections, of people? It would take quite
an act of courage to write a decidedly Protestant will when one's environment was essentially Catholic, or to be a stick-in-the-mud to the
old, outgrown spiritual forms of a moribund Catholicism in an environment of reformist fervor. Would not wills generally underestimate
the strength of Protestantism before Elizabeth and measure more
often older constituencies likely to be sympathetic to Catholicism?[15]

Local studies[16] provide local pictorial results and are not homogeneous in their response to change. In one case, the continuing
commitment of the region's population to its traditional rites on the
eve of the Reformation was beyond question so that the "changes
wrought in the next thirty years were all the more significant."[17] In
fact, as Henry's reign wore on there was a diminishing of investment
in traditional equipment required for traditional religious rites, and in
the reign of Edward, there was a wholesale collapse. Restoration under
Mary was only partial. But was this a signal of Protestant endorsement? Was it a conversion from Catholicism to Protestantism or
merely a transition from traditional commitments to passivity or
indifference? How, indeed, can such phenomena be discerned in
quantification?

In yet another local study, Susan Brigen's massive work on
London[18] strongly suggests a lively evangelical movement which had
begun in the mid 1530s and which was able to survive Henry's conservative reaction in his last years. Northumberland was convinced
that he had the support of the London evangelicals in both 1549 and
1553, yet London interestingly rallied behind Mary against Lady Jane.
But support soon waned and those "who kept faith through the dark
night of Mary's reign were able to draw on by now well-established
affinities" so that if they chose to remain in England they would be
protected, or if they opted to leave, their exile would be encouraged
with financial help.[19] Andrew Pettegree has made a fairly convincing
case to show that not enough attention has been given to the seeds of
reform during the reign of Mary which made the English church a
distinctive part of the European evangelical movement. The
reformers left behind and who did not escape into exile during Mary's
reign saw to it that the European dimension did not die with Mary's
accession. The celebrated trio of "Nicodemites," Parker, Cecil and
Elizabeth herself deserve as much credit for the shape of the
Elizabethan Settlement as those who traveled as refugees to the
Continent.[20]

It seems to the present author that England during the reign of
Mary was a very fractured society, and that thirty years of turmoil in
some localities, the same number of years of indifference or religious

transition in others, along with localities in the countryside which may have been clueless about what was going on in larger towns and university communities created a condition which was only exacerbated by the burning of over one hundred Protestants in and around London during Mary's reign—a condition which some Protestant reformers could not tolerate and thus left for exile in havens of Continental Protestantism. It may be that Protestantism, as a religion, was not solidified in England until the mid-years of Elizabeth's reign, and in this form we would surely need to call it Anglican, nevertheless enough destruction of the old ways had been accomplished that would prove decisive in determining the direction of the English Reformation. What ultimately would tell the tale during the reign of Elizabeth was the establishment of a Protestant clergy which encouraged the government to pursue a Protestant policy.[21]

The Marian exile was the focus of Christina Garrett's encyclopedic book published in 1938.[22] Her work has been the subject of many queries and controversies, and not a few historians have taken issue with her speculative conclusions. She became convinced that the Marian exiles, both in and out of Parliament, constituted a radical opposition party to Elizabeth, or, at the very least, leading intellectuals and gentry who favored the new religion and fled into exile during Mary Tudor's reign and who would ensure the future of English Protestantism "by keeping the flame of the new religion ablaze."[23] Because the exiles were predominantly a religious "party" when they left for exile in hopes of keeping English Protestantism alive during the resurgence of Catholicism, they returned under Elizabeth to become a political "party" to persuade the Queen to implement a more reformed and Protestant, indeed "purified" religious settlement.

J. E. Neale later seemed to augment Garrett's thesis by suggesting that a Puritan opposition composed mainly of former Marian exiles in Parliament obstructed the passage of the first supremacy bill of 1559, thus giving them a mandate to force the Queen to settle on a more radically Protestant church than she actually wanted.[24] This interpretation has been challenged by Norman Jones[25] and Kenneth Bartlett as well as a number of historians. Bartlett argues that there was no formal "program" which characterized the returning Marian exiles and that they did not set out to make it Parliament's business to establish "a godly polity in England based on continental models."[26] He points out as partial evidence that there was no unanimity among the exiles when they were on the Continent, and Geneva provided the fewest refugee members of Parliament although it represented the most radical group of Marian exiles. The Geneva refugees included a number of individuals from lower classes as well as quite a few women. Nevertheless, several Geneva exiles bear the names of later members of Parliament: John Bateman, Thomas Bodley, William Morley, John Pelham and Thomas Stanley. In stark contrast, the English exiles at Venice were more political refugees who were posturing themselves for important posts in Elizabeth's government. They were embarrassed by the likes of the Geneva refugees and their stringent calls for religious reform; most of the Marian exiles who would later serve in Parliament were motivated more by political than religious reasons for emigration. As a whole, Bartlett believes the Marian exiles were fairly conservative. Garrett and Neale were thus mistaken, although it is clear that their exile did give the refugees the sense of the place of England within history as canonized in John Foxe's *Acts and Monuments*.[27] The very disjunction evidenced in exile among the English Protestants, however, exemplified by the "Troubles at Frankfurt" as well as the tension between the Geneva exiles and those at Zurich and Basel, anticipated two halves of Elizabeth's reign: in the first half moderate puritans were represented in Parliament while the presbyterian opposition would be represented in Parliament during the second half of the reign.[28]

N. M. Sutherland has also been one of Garrett's more outspoken detractors, and his study of the Marian exiles is noteworthy for its comprehension and critical examination of the wider context of the Marian exile as it relates to government, the Parliament of 1559, and the new English church. Sutherland argues that the Marian exiles were not a homogeneous group, and that "there were clearly different sorts of 'exile'...."[29] Upon their return, those few who became members of the Parliament of 1559 constituted no "party, faction or cabal who, through determination and organisation, dominated the lower house and opposed the queen's more moderate policies," but rather were "men who could reasonably be expected by their patrons...to have supported and assisted the government, not least in its urgent, religious programme." Many of the clergy had been Edwardian divines and would be expected to proceed "from the Reformation programme previously enacted but barely executed by the time of Edward's death." Thus Garrett's contention that nearly all the exile clergy remained in disfavor and were sequestered for non-conformity is misleading, for it posits a puritanism in 1559 that is not distinguished from that of the 1570s onward. In fact, Sutherland says, there were no Puritans in 1559.[30]

Sutherland does not view the Convocation of 1563 as a demonstration of radical puritan sentiment. It might even be argued, he suggests, that "even the more radical elements" were "behind the settlement, except for various detailed interpretations relating to apparel, rites and ceremonies." These were "small things" which were considered much larger by certain conscientious and scrupulous minds, but in the end the Elizabethan Settlement formed the Anglican Church because of the bishops' acceptance of government authority: "Imperfect in their sight, it was still a wise and dignified achievement in war-torn Reformation Europe." Rather than Garrett's and Neale's radical puritan "party," Sutherland's exiles "emerge as generally temperate establishment men, whose opposition mainly consisted in getting away with local deviations," doing more to "assist the queen to fashion and enforce her Anglican settlement than they ever did to undermine it."[31]

Sutherland lumps all the exile communities together without regard for their geographical or ideological differences; any nuance of non-conformity save for the radical political thought of Knox and Goodman is missing from his analysis. Students of the Marian exile who have a keener appreciation for theology and religious discourse will not be helped by Sutherland's reductionist approach to such matters. The constant juxtaposition of "political" and "religious" refugee(s) in both Bartlett's and Sutherland's analyses is likewise confusing and in need of clarification. Other historians such as Rosemary O'Day and Patrick Collinson emphasize that Elizabeth's first bishops were persuaded to accept unpalatable religious practices as adiaphora because they believed that the Queen alone could secure the Reformation in England. They were convinced that their primary duty was preaching, and many "deplored the papistical trappings of episcopacy, hesitated about accepting bishoprics and declared progressive intentions."[32] Collinson refers to Elizabethan bishops who had returned from exile as "amphibians, partaking of both the official and unofficial reformations," and who promoted a religious policy "which was more their own than the Crown's and which partly derived from the unofficial Reformation."[33] The second generation of Elizabethan bishops, contrariwise, thought of themselves as defenders of the status quo against Catholics and Puritans alike; they stressed the bishops' disciplinary role and worked mainly as administrators. Few of the churchmen we will meet in this study had a problem with the supremacy of the Queen over the church as long as the monarchy was the bastion of true religion. It is neither necessary nor accurate, as characteristic of Sutherland's portrait, to depict the radical Marian exiles as proto-separatists. Moreover, Elizabeth's first generation of bishops reminded her of the limits of her power and the importance of obeying a higher power if necessary. Archbishop Grindal's unwillingness to stop the "prophesyings" in 1576 cost him his ecclesiastical post because he exhorted his Queen with due humility to approach the Almighty, *Non mea, sed tua voluntas fiat.*[34]

Elizabeth was forced to work with reformers as bishops before 1580, but from that point on she chose her bishops with the knowledge of Grindal's defection. It is doubtful that the returning exiles were suitable to her personal taste although she had little alternative but to use them. When she ascended the throne, "the problem was less one of a nonconforming than an absent clergy."[35] A decade or so later, she would have another generation of university-educated clerics who would be more to her liking. The key, of course, was not their Protestantism, but their willingness to back the status quo and deliver what the Crown found congenial.

Comprehensive research on the specific Marian exile community at Geneva is practically synonymous with the seminal work of Charles Martin, *Les Protestants Anglais réfugiés à Genève au temps de Calvin 1555–1560*. Nothing of its stature has been published since Martin's book appeared in 1915. S.J. Knox is the author of a Trinity College, Dublin thesis on the Geneva exiles,[36] and older studies may be found such as W.M. Southgate's probing the influence of Calvin on the Marian exiles at Geneva, as well as other exile communities,[37] and Henry Cowell's comprehensive article on the English-speaking refugee churches at Geneva and Frankfurt.[38] For more recent scholarly treatment on the Geneva exiles, readers must be content with rather piecemeal articles which focus on rather narrow or esoteric points of interest, many of which are cited in the chapters to follow.[39] Martin's book is not easily accessible to English readers and needs to be updated in light of more recent scholarship. The present study attempts to meet this need by providing a single volume on the Marian exiles who settled in Geneva, tracing the history of the church, examining its membership in detail, and collating the theology of the influential minds who resided there under Calvin's tutelage during the crucial years, 1555 to 1560.

Since this is a study in English Puritanism and its author uses the word "puritan" frequently, it will be necessary to indicate to the reader how the word is used; he does so with certain fear and trepidation and without any desire to engage in a taxonomy debate. "Puritan" is applied with a number of meanings and connotations and suffers, as Basil Hall suggests, like an erstwhile, useful coin from over-minting and inflation.[40] It seems that the word was not used before 1563, and there are not a few historians who wish that the term not be applied prior to the Act of Uniformity of 1559 at the earliest. Still, those who would be called such a name from 1559 onward were leading a protest, in the name of a more biblically grounded religion, against the Act of Uniformity and the episcopal enforcement of it. What about those engaged in a similar ideological war prior to 1559: what name should be given to them, many of whose ideas are highlighted in this volume? What seemed to be of utmost importance to these ante-Act of Uniformity Protestant reformers was their doctrine of the church, including ministry, preaching, ordination, ecclesiastical discipline of morality and the sacraments.[41] Put differently, we know that before 1642 the "serious" people in the Church of England who desired some modifications in church government and worship were indeed called "Puritans"; after 1640 the same "serious" people began to be called "Presbyterians," "Independents," or "Baptists." Prior to the 1640s, therefore, "puritan" could have several different meanings.

Peter Lake represents a number of recent scholars who do not find useful the dichotomy of puritans as Calvinist, congregationalist and anti-ceremonial versus Anglicans as Protestant but not Calvinist, episcopalian and ceremony- and sacrament-centered although in no sense crypto-popish, or in shorter version, Anglicanism as a kind of *via media* between Rome and Geneva.[42] The more radical Protestant reformers, from the inside looking out, referred to themselves as "the godly," whereas those from the outside looking in called them "puritans." Neither is "conformity" an especially helpful category for Lake, for a "conformist" during Elizabeth's early reign often referred to one who made a "polemical fuss" about the issues of church government, and not necessarily to those who conformed whose opposites were stigmatized as "puritans."

Matthew Parker, Archbishop of Canterbury under Elizabeth, used the term "puritan" only in November 1572, and before that he referred to these radical voices of reform as "recusants," "precisemen," or "precisians." Parker thought of them as subversive and innovative—"they can abide no superiority."[43] But puritans did not want to be known as schismatics or pure ones or even those who "were factious persons in the commonwealth." They wanted to be true to the faith, the faith of the primitive church as circumscribed in the Bible; they had no desire to be neutral in a faith which still carried vestiges of a church which had apostatized from its apostolic ideals. Thomas Cartwright did not like the word "puritan" as an epithet of this ethos believing it to be an invention of papists fostered by Whitgift-likes. Whitgift had charged the puritans with not laughing in their pharisaic smugness, but Cartwright answered that they were too sad to laugh at the dismal state of the Church of England. Besides, he chirked, "puritans" did indeed laugh even though they may not show their teeth![44]

H. C. Porter's useful taxonomy of Puritans includes: (1) Separatists who looked back to the Marian exiles and to the London secret churches under Mary and who continued that secret tradition in the 1560s; this was one of the foundations of the American experience; (2) "Evangelical Puritans" who wanted a more precise reformation but were part of the national church, Calvinist in theology but more emphatic "than official theology could approve of"; (3) the English tradition of rhetorical and radical "indignation and dissent" which included William Tyndale, John Bale and John Foxe, and which can be traced back to Lollardy; and (4) the "presbyterian attempt" in the 1570s and 1580s or the Puritan classis movement which was persuaded that the magistrate should be subject to the church and that the commonwealth must be suited to and governed by the church in perpetuity. This was the area which concerned prelates like Whitgift because it smacked of a revolutionary overthrow of the power of the civil magistrate in both ecclesiastical and civil matters, indeed a primary reason why Elizabethan prelates had such disdain for the Geneva exiles: it was precisely this kind of political theology which characterized at least two tyrannicidal tracts to come from the pens of two Geneva exiles, Christopher Goodman and John Knox.[45]

Thus the puritan ethos was not just theological or strictly religious, although it clearly was that; it was also socially disturbing. Nor was puritanism the purview of an intellectual elite and university-trained minds; the surplice was not just offensive to puritan clergy but among "simple gospelers" or ordinary folk. If there was one symbol of the puritan ethos it was the sermon, usually delivered for the most part by salaried lecturers rather than beneficed parsons, and whose connection to the established church always seemed tenuous. What puritans lacked in numbers they made up in both individual zeal and the disciplined strength of their communities. Within ten years of Elizabeth's accession, secretly and in defiance of the law, they were using among themselves orders of Reformed worship and discipline akin to those used publicly and with permission by the "stranger churches" such as John à Lasco's during the reign of Edward VI. Eighty years later, William Laud objected to the "stranger churches" for the distracting example they provided the English Puritans of the Stuart era.[46]

The present author has chosen herefrom to use the word "puritan" in small case by which is indicated a branch of English reformers who wanted England to become more Protestant and less Roman Catholic. Each classification in Porter's taxonomy would fit unless it makes no chronological sense. Some of the English exiles at Geneva would become part of the classis movement in the 1570s and 1580s; some might have been tempted to turn Separatist. But in the main, they were dissenters who wanted a more precise reformation of the national church, who sought to purify its doctrine, church polity and morality, and whose experience in exile gave impetus to their criticisms. The "theological, moral and social tensions"[47] of the subjects of the present study will be the test of their puritanism, "over-minted," "inflated" or whatever.

NOTES

[1] A. F. Pollard, *Henry VIII* (New York: Harper Torchbooks, 1966); *Thomas Cranmer and the English Reformation, 1489–1556* (London: Frank Cass, 1965); *Wolsey: Church and State in Sixteenth Century England* (New York: Harper Torchbooks, 1966).

[2] See Rosemary O'Day, *The Debate on the English Reformation* (London and New York: Methuen, 1986), p. 103.

[3] Among Elton's many writings, a place to begin is *England under the Tudors* (London: Methuen, 1955).

[4] O'Day, p. 120.

[5] See Joel Hurstfield (ed.), *The Reformation Crisis* (London: Arnold, 1965).

[6] See J. J. Scarisbrick, *Henry VIII* (London: Eyre and Spottiswoode, 1968), and *The Reformation and the English People* (Oxford: Blackwell, 1984).

[7] A. G. Dickens, *The English Reformation* (London: Collins, 1964), rev. Second Edition (University Park, Pennsylvania: Pennsylvania State University Press, 1989). Cf. Andrew Pettegree, "Re-Writing the English Reformation," *Nederlands Archief voor Kerkgeschiedenis* (1992), 37–58.

[8] See Christopher Haigh, "Some Aspects of the Recent Historiography of the English Reformation," *Stadtbürgertum und Adel in der Reformation: Studien zur Sozialgeschichte der Reformation in England und Deutschland*, ed. by Wolfgang J. Mommsen (Stuttgart: Klett-Cotta, 1979); *The English Reformation Revised* (Cambridge: University Press, 1987); "The Church of England, the Catholics and the People," *The Reign of Elizabeth I* (Athens: University of Georgia Press, 1985).

[9] *Reformation and Resistance in Tudor Lancashire* (Cambridge: University Press, 1975).

[10] In addition to his *The English Reformation,* one might consult also A. G. Dickens and Dorothy Carr, *The Reformation in England to the Accession of Elizabeth I* (London: Arnold, 1967), and J. F. Davies, *Heresy and Reformation in the South-East of England 1520–1559* (London: Royal Historical Society, 1983); cf. O'Day, pp. 138–39.

[11] O'Day, pp. 138ff. In this context, cf. Clare Cross, *Church and People 1450–1660* (London: Fontana, 1976), whose documentation stresses the changes in the laity as a result of the Reformation and seems therefore to be a problem for the Scarisbrick-Haigh interpretation.

[12] S. T. Bindoff, *Tudor England* (London: Penguin, 1964).

[13] Scarisbrick, *The Reformation and the English People.*

[14] See O'Day, pp. 149ff.

[15] *Ibid.*, pp. 156–58; cf. Pettegree, "Re-Writing the English Reformation."

[16] E.g., Robert Whiting, *The Blind Devotion of the People. Popular Religion and the English Reformation* (Cambridge: University Press, 1989); Peter Clark, *English Provincial Society from the Reformation to the Revolution.*

Religion, Politics and Society in Kent, 1500–1640 (Hassocks, Sussex: Harvester, 1977); Margaret Bowker, *The Secular Clergy in the Diocese of Lincoln, 1495–1520* (Cambridge: University Press, 1969).

[17]Pettegree, "Re-Writing the English Reformation," p. 45.

[18]Susan Brigen, *London and the Reformation* (Oxford: University Press, 1989).

[19]Pettegree, "Re-Writing the English Reformation," p. 48.

[20]Andrew Pettegree, *Marian Protestantism: Six Studies.* (Hampshire, England: Scolar Press, 1996), p. 6.

[21]Pettegree, "Re-Writing the English Reformation"; O'Day, pp. 156–66.

[22]C. H. Garrett, *The Marian Exiles. A Study in the Origins of Elizabethan Puritanism* (Cambridge: University Press, 1938).

[23]O'Day, p. 153; cf. Frederick A. Norwood, "The Marian Exiles—Denizens or Sojourners? *Church History* 13 (1944), 100–10. See also N. M. Sutherland, "The Marian Exiles and the Establishment of the Elizabethan Regime," *Archiv für Reformationsgeschichte* 78 (1987), 253–84.

[24]J. E. Neale, "The Elizabethan Acts of Supremacy and Uniformity," *English Historical Review* 65 (1950), 304–32; cf. Sutherland, "The Marian Exiles and the Establishment of the Elizabethan Regime."

[25]Norman L. Jones, *Faith by Statute. Parliament and the Settlement of Religion, 1559* (London: Royal Historical Society, 1982).

[26]Kenneth R. Bartlett, "The Role of the Marian Exiles," in P. W. Hasler, *The House of Commons 1558–1603* (London: The History of Parliament Trust, 1981), I, 102–10.

[27]*Ibid.* See Sutherland, "The Marian Exiles and the Establishment of the Elizabethan Regime."

[28]Bartlett, "The Role of the Marian Exiles."

[29]Sutherland, "The Marian Exiles and the Establishment of the Elizabethan Regime," p. 284. The present author's criticism of Sutherland's case is adumbrated further in chapter three.

[30]*Ibid.*, pp. 258–68.

[31]*Ibid.*, pp. 277–82.

[32]O'Day, p. 176.

[33]Patrick Collinson, "The Elizabethan Church and the New Religion," *The Reign of Elizabeth I*, p. 177.

[34]O'Day, p. 189; Collinson, "The Elizabethan Church and the New Religion," pp. 185ff.

[35]O'Day, *ibid.*

[36]Samuel James Knox, "A Study of the Genevan Exiles and their Influence upon the Rise of Nonconformity in England" (Trinity College, Dublin, 1953). See also Knox's brief abstract of his thesis in *John Knox's Genevan Congregation* (The Presbyterian Historical Society of England, 1956).

[37]W. M. Southgate, "The Marian Exiles and the Influence of John Calvin," *History* 27 (1942), 148–52.

[38]Henry J. Cowell, "The Sixteenth-century English-speaking Refugee Churches at Geneva and Frankfort," *Proceedings of the Huguenot Society of Great Britain and Ireland* 16 (1939), 209–30.

[39]Some examples include O. T. Hargrave, "The Predestinarian Offensive of the Marian Exiles at Geneva," *Historical Magazine of the Protestant Episcopal Church* 42 (1973), 111–23; Richard Bauckham, "Marian Exiles and Cambridge Puritanism: James Pilkington's 'Halfe a Score'," *Journal of Ecclesiastical History* 26 (1975), 137–48; and, Ronald J. VanderMolen, "Anglican Against Puritan: Ideological Origins during the Marian Exile," *Church History* 42 (1973), 45–57.

[40]Basil Hall, "Puritanism: the Problem of Definition," *Studies in Church History* II (1965), 283–96.

[41]Hall, *Ibid.* Cf. Paul Christenson, "Reformers and the Church of England under Elizabeth I and the Early Stuarts," *Journal of Ecclesiastical History* 31 (1980) 463–87, and Patrick Collinson, "A Comment: Concerning the Name Puritan," in the same number of the *Journal of Ecclesiastical History,* 488.

[42]Peter Lake, *Anglicans and Puritans? Presbyterianism and English Conformist Thought from Whitgift to Hooker* (London: Hyman, 1988), p. 5.

[43]Parker, *Correspondence* (Parker Society), p. 434, quoted in H. C. Porter, *Puritanism in Tudor England* (London: Macmillan, 1970), p. 5.

[44]See Porter, *Puritanism in Tudor England,* p. 3.

[45]*Ibid.*

[46]Patrick Collinson, *Godly People. Essays on English Protestantism and Puritanism* (London: Hambledon Press, 1983), pp. 9ff. Cf. Thomas Clancy, S.J., "Papist-Protestant-Puritan: English Religious Taxonomy 1565–1665," *Recusant History* 13 (1976), 227–53.

[47]Collinson, *ibid.*

CHAPTER 1

HISTORICAL BACKGROUND OF THE GENEVA EXILES, 1555 TO 1560

Edward VI died on 6 July 1553 at the age of fifteen. The Duke of Northumberland, who earlier had unseated the Duke of Somerset as advisor and protector to the king, was influential in getting his daughter-in-law, Lady Jane Grey, named successor to the throne. But she and Northumberland were killed, and the Protestant Archbishop of Canterbury, Thomas Cranmer, was imprisoned. The events signaling a reformation of religion in England thus took a drastically new direction. The nation which had made many changes in the direction of the religion of Continental Protestantism would seek to retrench its identity as a Catholic nation, that is, a *Roman* Catholic nation. The changes would be effectuated by the coronation of Mary Tudor as monarch of England. She was crowned queen in October of 1553; as early as August she made it known publicly that she was Catholic but that she had no desire to force or restrain other forms of religion. The "public order fixed by common accord," however, spelled bad news for Protestant reformers in England. Many of them, including Cranmer, Nicholas Ridley, Miles Coverdale and Hugh Latimer, both bishops and preachers alike, were either deposed or imprisoned. Privileges granted to foreigners who had been invited to assist in the reformation of religion and society during Edward's time were revoked, although the foreign refugees were guaranteed safe-conducts back to their homelands. John à Lasko, the superintendent of the Polish refugee church in London, left in September with a band of his parishioners for Denmark, eventually finding a home in Emden. Peter Martyr Vermigli, invited by Cranmer to teach religion at Oxford, returned to Strasburg. Others followed suit.

Mary's legitimacy was returned to her by Parliament when she was proclaimed rightful heir of Henry VIII. Parliament, as it had done with her predecessors, gave her supremacy over ecclesiastical matters which Mary used two months after her coronation to restore the mass. Her marriage to Philip II of Spain caused public unrest, and revolts broke out such as the one led by Sir Thomas Wyatt in 1554. Persecutions of Protestants began in earnest, and by the last months of 1554, England had been legally reconciled with Rome. England was to be Roman Catholic again.[1]

Many English people planned to leave their homeland for fear of persecution. It is estimated that some eight-hundred Protestants fled for refuge on the Continent.[2] Important names surface among the Marian exiles: Alexander Nowell, Edwin Sandys, Edmund Grindal, Thomas Cole, John Ponet, Sir John Cheke, Sir Anthony Cooke and Sir Richard Morrison went to Strasburg to join Peter Martyr; others were attracted to Zurich where Heinrich Bullinger hailed—these included Lawrence Humphrey, John Parkhurst, James Pilkington, Thomas Bentham, Richard Horne, Thomas Lever, Richard Chambers and William Cole. John Bale went to Basel where he published in 1557 his catalogue of famous British writers. John Foxe was also at Basel where he would be collecting data for his influential martyrology, *Acts and Monuments.* The Duke and Duchess of Suffolk found refuge at Emden, then Weinheim and finally Poland.[3]

In Frankfurt, the Marian exiles included a group of Flemish weavers which had been planted in Glastonbury by Somerset and had been supervised by Valerand Poullain. Poullain had succeeded Calvin at Strasburg as minister for the French congregation. The interesting feature of the Flemish refugees in England was that, like the London "Church of the Foreigners" under the supervision and pastoral care of John à Lasko, they were given autonomy to plan and implement their own form of worship and church polity without interference from English bishops. As such, they became a mirror of a "more reformed" England in the minds of Protestants who, later during the Elizabethan Settlement, would look back and remind the Queen and her bishops of what was permitted, even endorsed by the government.[4]

The Poullain entourage had been welcomed by John Glauberg, a local Frankfurt nobleman, city councilor and friend of John Calvin. On 15 May 1554, the Walloons were granted the use of Weissfrauen Kirke, and Poullain began work on a liturgy, one which in substance had already been used at Glastonbury, which he presented to the Frankfurt city council. Translated into Latin, the preface of the church order indicated that the spirit of the liturgy was to emulate the simplicity of the presbyterian order found in the New Testament, and that should differences of opinion arise over the contents of the order, leading members of the Reformed faith would corroborate its faithfulness to apostolic Christian practice. Poullain added a Latin translation of a 1552 Confession of Faith originally written in French. The carefully arranged collection was signed by Poullain and the elders of his church.[5]

It is unclear what happened to the document, for when it finally appeared before the city council on 1 September 1554, it bore also the names of four Englishmen and a Scot: John Staunton, William Hammond, John Bendall, William Whittingham, and John MacBray. Obviously, these men were refugees from Marian England who also had sought asylum in Frankfurt. Some two hundred refugees had arrived in Frankfurt on 2 June, led by Edmond Sutton, William Williams, Whittingham, and Thomas Wood, and were welcomed by Poullain and his company. The English exiles obtained the same privileges from the Frankfurt authorities as the French enjoyed including the use of the same church building. The one stipulation given them was that their worship and doctrinal stance remain in essence the same as the French, and they could easily substantiate the congruity with their fellow refugees by signing their Confession of Faith.[6] William Whittingham subsequently drew up a church order of worship for the English congregation which differed from the 1552 Prayerbook; the litany, surplice and other details were omitted.

The heart of the service was a revised confession of faith, a metered psalm sung a cappella by the congregation, a prayer for the assistance of the Holy Spirit, and the sermon. This was followed by the Lord's Prayer, the recitation of the creed, another sung psalm, and the benediction. The English church order also provided for ecclesiastical discipline, that is, rules for members of the church as well as church leaders. Public confession of the faith before the elders and ministers of the church was required of each member of the congregation; if any were unacceptable to the elders and ministers, they were subject to discipline until they repented. All church meetings had to be attended, and young people were required to receive catechetical instruction. The official positions of leadership in the church were a pastor or superintendent, preachers, elders and deacons; these were exactly the same positions which had been utilized in the à Lasko and Poullain churches in London during Edward's reign. John MacBray, the Scot, was elected the preacher, and the first service was held on 29 July 1554.[7]

None of the other refugee communities had attained such good
fortune in their home away from home. The use of the Weissfrauen
Kirke had been very helpful in making the adjustment to a new and
different environment. Exercising their good fortune, the English
exiles in Frankfurt wrote a letter to the other refugee communities—
Emden, Zurich, Strasburg and Wesel—to explain how they had obtained their fortunate circumstances, and to invite them to come and
join them at Frankfurt to form a strong and vibrant church which
would be established on Reformed principles. This exile church should
become exemplary of what a reformed church should be to those back
home in England.[8] The letter did not have the desired results. The
refugees at Strasburg interpreted it as an invitation to provide a superintendent for the Frankfurt church, and they named four possible
candidates: John Ponet, John Scory, John Bale, and Richard Cox. In
fact, Edmund Grindal, the future Elizabethan bishop and Archbishop
of Canterbury, sent word to Scory, then at Emden, urging him to
accept. But the Frankfurt church had not intended the letter to be an
invitation to provide a superintendent, and they promptly elected
three pastors, Thomas Lever, James Haddon (who refused to serve)
and John Knox, who by that time had reached Geneva from Dieppe
and was being championed by Calvin.

When the same letter reached the refugees at Zurich they delayed
a response until 13 October 1554, finally indicating that their intentions were to stay in Zurich to study with Bullinger; they could, they
responded further, come by the next Easter should the invitation still
be open provided that they could continue to worship according to
the Second Edwardian Prayerbook, "for we are fully determined to
admit and use no other."[9]

Before they had received Zurich's delayed response, the English
refugees at Frankfurt sent a follow-up letter to Zurich. In response,
the exiles in Zurich dispatched Richard Chambers, a wealthy and well-
respected member of the Zurich group, to Frankfurt. Knox had
arrived in Frankfurt in the meantime, and when Chambers arrived, he
was told by the English exiles of Frankfurt how they were committed
to remain faithful to the arrangements they had made with the
Frankfurt authorities. They would be glad to use the Prayerbook, they
said, "so far as God's word doth commend it," but there were
"ceremonies" in it which they did not intend to use. Chambers left for
Strasburg, and two weeks later returned to Frankfurt with Grindal with
the intention of requesting the city council to allow the English
church the use of the Prayerbook. They were afraid, they lamented,

that failure to use the English Prayerbook would offend and demean their brothers and sisters of the faith who were imprisoned in England. Discussion between Grindal, Knox and Whittingham ensued, and the future Archbishop was forced to admit that there might be some objectionable items in the Prayerbook, but that it should be adhered to "in substance and effect." Knox adumbrated his objections to private baptisms, the churching of women and certain language of the litany, especially the words "by Thine Agony and bloody sweat."[10] But no meeting of the minds resulted. Grindal and Chambers then asked the Frankfurt authorities for a separate church building in which to meet, only to be told that this was impossible as long as the Diet of Augsburg was in session. They then left Frankfurt to return to Strasburg.

The Knox and Whittingham refugees had asked to send along with them a letter explaining their position regarding their reservations about the Prayerbook. The English Frankfurters were somewhat naive; they believed that their reservations about the Prayerbook would not cause division among the English Protestant congregations on the Continent. But the cleavage between the Frankfurt church and the other refugee churches was serious, and the former's goal of setting up an exemplary national church in exile was laid to rest by 13 December 1554.[11] Left to themselves, the Frankfurt refugees turned their attention to the implementation of a new church order. They thought initially of implementing the 1545 liturgy of Geneva which had recently been made available in English in 1550, and a committee was established to study the matter. But Knox expressed his reservation about implementing a new church order without input from other English refugee communities. He raised his objections to the Edwardian Prayerbook, however, and requested permission to preach only and to allow others to administer the sacraments. His request was denied, and he would have resigned as minister but for the refusal of the congregation to accept it.

Finally Thomas Lever arrived from Zurich to assume his elected duties as pastor with Knox. Lever attempted to overcome the impasse with the suggestion of adopting yet another church order independent of both Swiss and English models. Most of the congregation were not persuaded by Lever's suggestion, and the Frankfurt church decided to enlist Calvin's help. An abstract of the Second Edwardian Prayerbook was sent to him, and Knox wrote letters to his fellow ministers to encourage Calvin to give it careful scrutiny. Knox even volunteered to leave Frankfurt to continue his studies in Geneva, thus removing himself from the skirmish for the good of the cause. Calvin's response, a "club of Hercules" to the author of the *Troubles at Frankfurt,* was somewhat predictable: he saw more than a few remnants of the old, objectionable religion which should be removed in time, but they could be tolerated for a season.[12]

Finally, after Anthony Gilby implored for resolution on his knees, a liturgy was assimilated by Knox and Whittingham representing one side, and Lever and Thomas Perry the other. The compromise order was to be used until the last of April, and any questions or objections were to be referred to five leading Reformed theologians for arbitration: Calvin, Bullinger, Martyr, Musculus and Viret. Matters seemed to be working peacefully until 13 March 1555, when Richard Cox brought a new group of English refugees to Frankfurt. This event was to disrupt the Frankfurt refugee church to the point of division, and the more radical members of the Frankfurt church would seek asylum elsewhere.[13]

The "Liturgy of Compromise" as it has become labeled, was based on the Second Edwardian Prayerbook with certain modifications. There were no congregational responses, for example, and only the Lord's Prayer and Apostles' Creed were recited by the congregation. The collects and special prayers were eliminated, and the litany, said by the minister without response by the congregation, was made optional. Christmas, Easter, Ascension, Pentecost, and Feast Days of the Saints were absent. The communion service remained fairly in tact but the congregation likely did not kneel before the altar-table. Private baptisms were removed, as were godparents' responses in behalf of infants—the parents, instead, affirmed in their own name to raise their children in the nurture and admonition of the Lord. No sign of the cross was allowed in marking the infant, and confirmation by a bishop was deemed unnecessary. Catechetical instruction to each child was mandatory before the child could receive communion; this began with a doctrinal exposition on baptism and the new birth and continued with the Decalogue, the Apostles' Creed and the "Our Father" with accompanying commentary. The ring was excluded from the marriage rite as was the father giving his daughter in marriage. The Prayerbook was made optional for the visitation of the sick and the funeral service. An order of ecclesiastical discipline was added. Provisions were made for the election of ministers, elders and deacons. The church order concluded with two prayers, one inspired by persecution contained intercession for prisoners, martyrs and exiles, the other for King Philip and Queen Mary that their hearts might be softened so that they could become defenders of the gospel.[14]

When Cox and the newer English refugees attended the service and uttered aloud responses as indicated in the Prayerbook, they were reminded of the newly accepted compromise liturgy. They answered that they were doing only what they had done in church back home in England, and that any worshipping community of English people should reflect the face of an English church. Knox's response was that the church should reflect the face of Christ's church! On the following Sunday morning one of the newcomers, John Jewel, stalwart apologist for English Protestantism who had escaped England after signing the Catholic articles, read the English litany. In the afternoon, Knox preached a sermon in which he leveled his criticism of the Prayerbook. Emotions raged hot until Glauberg attempted to reconcile the various factions among the English refugees. His attempt seemed to be working until some of Knox's writings, principally his *Faithful Admonition*, were shown to the Frankfurt authorities by members of the Cox party. The citations were ominous, for they spoke disparagingly of not only Philip II, Mary and her officers, but of Charles V, likening him to Nero. The emperor was then at Augsburg, and the Frankfurt city council could ill-afford further difficulties. Knox was asked to leave. He left soon thereafter on 26 March, less than two weeks of the arrival of the Cox party.[15]

The rift between the two parties was not only serious but portended a serious division within the Elizabethan Settlement. On the one hand, Cox and his party represented a nationalist and royalist persuasion, a Protestantism which would well have received support from their fellow exiles in Zurich and Strasburg, places of exile on the Continent which housed future Elizabethan bishops and important officials of government. On the other hand, the radical group personified by Knox with support from Whittingham and others who preceded him at Frankfurt represented what they felt was an international form of Protestantism, a theological ethos founded on the rock of primitive apostolic Christianity. They were convinced that Edwardian Protestants would have been part of an international Protestant movement of reform had they been granted due time. The focus of the issues which divided the two parties was the Prayerbook, but the issues went much deeper and were to become seedbed for later puritan furor of the radical wing of that immensely pluralistic English Protestant tradition.[16]

With Knox gone, the Cox party pursued the course of creating an English refugee church based on the Second Edwardian Prayerbook with vigilance. Adolphus von Glauberg, the nephew of John Glauberg, supported the Coxians in the fracas and gave notification to Whittingham. John Glauberg became convinced that he should be of the same mind and posture as his nephew. For Whittingham, the rules of the game had been changed, and he asked permission to join some other church, perhaps Poullain's, but his request was denied. The Cox party held a new election where only priests and ministers could vote; Christopher Goodman, an ardent supporter of Knox and Whittingham throughout the troubles, remonstrated but he was overruled. Interestingly, the Frankfurt authorities called for a lay vote among those English refugees who would sign the Forty-two Articles. A number of them refused to sign the Articles thus giving the Cox party clear sailing to win the election. David Whitehead was voted to fill the office of pastor temporarily, and two ministers, four elders and two deacons were elected. Letters were sent to Calvin and the imprisoned bishop, Nicholas Ridley, which whitewashed the whole affair.[17] In the letters, the Coxians contended that their demeanor was motivated by love for their country, although they did not "entertain any regard for our country which is not agreeable to God's holy word." The behavior of Knox, Whittingham and the other radicals, however, was "altogether a disgrace to their country."[18]

But Whittingham had already written to Calvin the day Knox had left Frankfurt giving his side of the story. The Genevan became upset about what had transpired, especially the way Knox was treated, and he expressed his displeasure with Cox and his followers. Whittingham was convinced that he and those members of the original group of Frankfurt exiles had to leave, and several members were sent in search of another city, such as Zurich, Basel or Geneva, in which to worship. This information was given to Whitehead who responded by calling Whittingham and his sympathizers schismatic; they were pressed with the question of why they felt compelled to leave Frankfurt. Their answer was in the form of seven reasons the essence of which was that changes in what had been agreed upon in the liturgy resulted in "papistical superstitions" and "useless ceremonies" yoked upon the whole congregation.[19] On 27 August 1555, the Whittingham party demanded the appointment of two arbitrators on each side of the dispute to settle the question of the legality of their departure. Nothing came of this, angry words were exchanged, and toward the end of September, "in some heat they departed."[20]

As early as 10 June 1555, close to the time Whittingham had been in Geneva in search for a new church-home, Calvin appeared before the city council of Geneva to inform them that "certain Englishmen are desirous to repair hither for the sake of the Word of God" and to request that the council provide a place where they could preach the gospel and administer the sacraments.[21] The council agreed to Calvin's request upon the condition that he be consulted. The churches of St. Germaine and Notre Dame la Neuve apparently had been suggested as possible locations, but nothing further happened until the English exiles appeared on 13 October.[22] On 24 October, Calvin appeared before the city council to remind them of their decision on behalf of the English company by reporting that "at other times these English had received other nations and given them churches, but now it has pleased God to afflict them." Three syndics were commissioned to study the matter and report back to the council on 14 November. Consequently, the council decided to grant to the English refugees cohabitation with Italian immigrants of the church of Marie la Nove, at the southeast corner of Cathedral Square, better known as the Auditoire, the famous lecture hall where Calvin delivered many of his sermons and lectures.

On 25 November Calvin again appeared before the council to assist in working out the details. The agreement was that the Italian refugees would have their church services on Thursdays, Fridays and Saturdays, and the English would have Mondays, Tuesdays and Wednesdays; both groups would share Sundays, the Italians at their accustomed hour and the English at nine in the morning. The minister of the church had to been chosen by the congregation, then present himself to the city council for approval. On 29 November 1555, Anthony Gilby and Christopher Goodman were chosen and took the required oath. It was here "that Puritanism was organized as a distinct school, if not also a distinct party in the church."[23] Indeed, it would be from Geneva that theological and political writings would flow, writings of a distinct if not radical nature; translations of the Bible, especially an annotated version which would leave a literary and theological legacy almost unparalleled by any other English Bible; a church order encasing the ideas labeled later as "precisian," "Genevan," and "Gospeler" would provide wide public debate; metrical psalms and a version of the English Psalter which even today inspire devotion; and, the many letters these exiles wrote in reflection of their own theological understanding and spiritual pilgrimage as followers of Jesus

Christ—all give a unique portrait of the mind and institutions of puritanism.

On 21 September Whittingham had written to Calvin from Frankfurt that the furniture was packed and sent off, and that he and his associates would soon follow. Some of Whittingham's group followed Foxe to Basel, but most of them came to Geneva. They arrived, as noted above, on 13 October, and the *Livre des Anglois* recorded that the English church was officially established on 1 November 1555. The church was provided a bell, a pulpit and benches. Although forty-seven persons were mentioned at its founding, one-hundred-thirty-nine others were added later during the Marian period, and twenty-six more were members briefly at one time or another. Almost a fourth of the Marian exiles, therefore, came under Genevan influence during the critical years 1555 to 1560.[24]

NOTES

[1]M. M. Knappen, *Tudor Puritanism* (Chicago: University of Chicago Press, 1939), p. 104; A. G. Dickens, *The English Reformation* (New York: Schocken Books, 1964), pp. 344–49, *passim*. Cf. the second edition of Dickens' monumental work (University Park: The Pennsylvania State University Press, 1989) which is the substance of the 1964 work with a few added chapters.

[2]Christina H. Garrett, *The Marian Exiles. A Study in the Origins of Elizabethan Puritanism* (Cambridge: University Press, 1938), p. 32; cf. John Foxe, *Acts and Monuments*, ed. Stephen R. Cattley (London: Seeley and Burside, 1837), VI, 430.

[3]See Garrett, *passim*.

[4]Charles Martin, *Les Protestants Anglais réfugiés à Genève au temps de Calvin 1555–1560* (Geneva: A. Jullian, 1915), p. 22; cf. John Bale, *Scriptorum illustrium maioris Brytanniae...*(Basel, 1557–59).

[5]Patrick Collinson, *Godly People. Essays on English Protestantism and Puritanism* (London: The Hambledon Press, 1983), pp. 246–54; Frederick A. Norwood, "The Strangers' 'Model Churches' in Sixteenth Century England," *Reformation Studies. Essays in Honor of Roland H. Bainton* (Richmond: John Knox Press, 1962), pp. 184–85.

[6]Martin, pp. 22–23.

[7]*Ibid.*, p. 23.

[8]Knappen, pp. 119–120.

[9]Knappen, as well as other readers, regards the letter as peremptory, using language which seemed to elevate the Frankfurt refugees above their brethren for having established a more reformed, apostolically verifiable church; pp. 119–120. See *A Brieff Discours off the Troubles Begonne at Franckford, 1554–1558 A.D.* (London: Elliot Stock, 1575), p. 29 (hereafter cited *Troubles*). The authorship of this account has been ascribed to William Whittingham (e.g. A. W. Pollard and G. R. Redgrave, *A Short Title Catalogue of Books Printed in England, Scotland and Ireland ...1475–1640* [London: Bernard Quaritch Ltd., 1926]), but Patrick Collinson has made a good case for Thomas Wood as the author. Collinson, "The Authorship of *A Brieff Discours off the Troubles Begonne at Franckford*," *Journal of Ecclesiastical History* 9 (1958), 188–209.

[10]*Troubles*, p. 37.

[11]*Ibid.*, pp. 37–38; David Laing, *The Works of John Knox* (Edinburgh: James Thin, 1895), IV, 61.

[12]Knappen, pp. 124–26. Martin suggests that the draft sent to Calvin was a bogus rendition, but no evidence is available to ascertain whether this is accurate. See Martin, p. 27.

[13]Martin, p. 27, Knappen, p. 126, and W. D. Maxwell, *John Knox's Genevan Service Book, 1556* (Edinburgh: Oliver and Boyd, 1931), p. 12.

[14]Martin, pp. 28–30.

[15]See Philip E. Hughes, *The Reformation in England,* Rev. Ed. (London: Burns and Oates, 1963), II, 315, and Knappen, pp. 128–29.

[16]See Ronald J. VanderMolen, "Anglican Against Puritan: Ideological Origins During the Marian Exile," *Church History* 42 (1973), 45–57. VanderMolen takes issue with Christina Garrett's claim that the Knoxians were more democratic and represented a lower social status. He argues, instead, for a difference in the appreciation of humanism, suggesting that the Coxians fostered a kind of humanism whereas the Knoxians represented a "death knell" to humanist scholarship. The Knoxian concern for implementation of biblical or apostolic primitivism forced them to become perfectionistic and negated a sense of historical conditioning which was at the heart of the humanist enterprise. While I appreciate VanderMolen's critique of Garrett, I do not find very persuasive the juxtaposition of biblical primitivist hermeneutics and humanist scholarship. The record of the exiles who settled in Geneva after the troubles at Frankfurt would clearly vindicate their scholarly concerns and talents. VanderMolen has keenly addressed the essence of the difference between what he calls "Anglican" and "Puritan" ideology, but the ideology must be researched as reflected in hermeneutics rather than attitudes toward humanist scholarship. VanderMolen's later study, "Providence as Mystery, Providence as Revelation: Puritan and Anglican Modifications of John Calvin's Doctrine of Providence," *Church History* 47 (1978), 27–47, seems to me to modify his earlier position somewhat, although the focus is given a larger context in which Calvin, Anglican and Puritan hermeneutics are perceptively compared and contrasted.

[17]Knappen, pp. 130–32.

[18]*Troubles*, p. 88. Cf. *Original Letters Relative to the English Reformation …from the Archives of Zurich*, ed. for the Parker Society by Hastings Robinson (Cambridge: University Press, 1846), II, 755–63 (hereafter cited *Zurich Letters*).

[19]*Troubles*, pp. 78–80; Martin, pp. 36–37.

[20]*Troubles*, pp. 81–85.

[21]A. F. Mitchell, ed., *Livre des Anglois or Register of the English Church at Geneva under the Pastoral Care of Knox and Goodman 1555–1559* (no date), p. 3.

[22]The *Livre des Anglois,* a record of their experiences bequeathed to the city council of Geneva upon their departure from Geneva in 1560, and a kind of "data-base" for the individual and collective church life during their stay, indicates that some English refugees had already been in Geneva before 13 October 1555.

[23]Mitchell, pp. 3ff.

[24]Martin points to 29 November 1555 as the date the church began, based on the Registres de Conseil of Geneva; see Martin, pp. 40–47; cf. Knappen, p. 142. Cowell numbered the persons exiled in Geneva at two-hundred-twelve individuals and one-hundred-forty-six families between 29 March 1555 and 28 October 1559. Forty-four had applied for citizenship by 14 October 1557. See Henry J. Cowell, "Sixteenth-Century English-speaking Refugee Churches at Geneva and Frankfort," *Proceedings of the Huguenot Society of London* XVI (1939), 209–30.

CHAPTER 2

EARLIEST MEMBERS OF THE GENEVA REFUGEE CHURCH

B efore they left Geneva on 30 May 1560, the English refugees bequeathed to the city a document of their own composition entitled, *Livre des Anglois or Register of the English Church at Geneva under the pastoral care of Knox and Goodman 1555–1559.* It became part of the Geneva register and was preserved in the Hotel de Ville, bound in parchment, with a parchment mark attached to the first leaf of each of its five parts. The pages were numbered 1 to 149, and a number were left blank after the entries in each of the five parts, perhaps indicating that the exiles thought their stay might be elongated. The authorship of the document is not known, although Knox and Whittingham have both been conjectured as the author. It seems more likely that Whittingham was the author, and at least "one expert thought the writing had less resemblance to that of Knox than of Whittingham."[1] He was in Geneva longer than Knox, was one of the last of the English refugees to leave the city, and was among those who presented the book as a memorial. The English thanked their hosts of the city council and pleaded to be retained as humble members of the Seigneurie, requesting an attestation of their life and conduct while they had resided in the city. Geneva granted them an honorable dismissal "and an attestation of the contentment we have with them...that they be exhorted to pray for us, and to do for strangers among themselves as others have done to them."[2]

The following two chapters will attempt to bring together a collective portrait of the Geneva English church. I will, at some risk to be sure, select pertinent names which appear in the *Livre des Anglois* and highlight the individual careers of these English Protestants before they went into exile, during the course of their stay in Geneva, and look forward to their activities, religious and otherwise, during the reign of Elizabeth. The selection of individual names is motivated by certain criteria: how long they stayed in Geneva; the amount of information which is ascertainable; their contributions to the Church of England in some discernible way; and, particularly whether and to what extent they may have played a role in the puritan movement.

It will come as no surprise that the familiar names of those whose activities were so pivotal in the "Troubles at Frankfurt" and the decision to move to Geneva will dominate our portrait. In some cases, particularly that of John Knox, their careers are well known or have been given recent treatment.[3] Those who wrote theological treatises, published sermons, translated biblical commentaries or wrote prefaces to religious and political tracts, and were actively engaged in substantive correspondence will be especially difficult to slight. These are the tools with which the intellectual historian or historical theologian works. The question remains, of course, whether they are adequate to present a clear and accurate picture of who these English refugees were and what precisely constituted their life together. If we presuppose that historians judge the past on the basis of people acting out their ideas, and that beliefs are what constitute ultimate concerns, our portrait can be a significant mirror of early sixteenth century puritanism.

I. ENGLISH EXILES IN GENEVA PRIOR TO THE ESTABLISHMENT OF THE CHURCH

The *Livre des Anglois* recorded that the first company of English refugees "as have bene receyved and admytted into the Englishe Churche and Congregation at Geneva" came on 13 October 1555, "to use the benefit of the Churche then newely graunted." There were some English refugees already in Geneva before this date. The names recorded in the *Livre des Anglois* began with Sir **William Stafford,** his wife, **Dorothee,** his sister, **Jane,** a mistress, **Sandes**, a cousin, **Ffoster**, and his children, **Edward** and **Elizabeth**. Servants and a maid were also recorded. Sir William was in Geneva as early as 29 March 1555, and was doubtless the wealthiest and most influential of the exiles. He was allowed, as a singular privilege, to wear his sword. He died while exiled in Geneva and was buried on 5 May 1556. His wife, Dorothee, gave birth to another son, **John,** while in Geneva; John was baptized on 4 January 1556. A controversy arose between Calvin who was named godfather to the child and Lady Dorothee. Calvin would not consent to allow the widow to leave with her children until he was assured that young John would be brought up a Protestant. The Stafford family left Geneva in 1558, and Lady

Stafford eventually became one of the Ladies of the Bedchamber to Queen Elizabeth.[4]

In addition to the Staffords, **Thomas Lever, John Prettie, Nicholas Harvye, Michael Gill, William Beauvoir, Harry Dunce, John Pigeon, William Amondesham,** and **Richard Amondesham** were named as having dwelt at Geneva before 13 October 1555. **Thomas Lever** is the most intriguing name in this list. Lever was educated at St. John's College, Cambridge and became Master of the college in 1551–1553. He had been widely recognized as a preacher, having preached before Edward VI at Paul's Cross in 1550. He supported the cause of Lady Jane Grey, but when Mary ascended to the throne, he went into exile with a number of student proteges from Cambridge and Oxford. He went first to Strasburg, then to Zurich before he came to Geneva on 7 April 1554 to hear Calvin lecture and preach.[5] He was in Zurich again in October, 1554, for he wrote a letter to John Bradford which gave a fairly extensive account of his travels and impressions of Reformed theologians during the troublesome months of that year. At some point, he returned to Geneva before joining the English refugees at Frankfurt as pastor in January of 1555. Knox had spoken favorably of Lever in his *Godly Letter sent to the Faithful in London,* but in Frankfurt the two did not get along. Lever attempted to introduce his own rendition of the Prayerbook which he avowed was neither Swiss nor English, but it was not accepted by the congregation. Knox blamed Lever for pushing Cox and Jewell into the Frankfurt fracas, thus helping to create further disruption when matters seemed to have settled into a peaceful resolution. Lever was in Strasburg during the winter of 1555–56, and in Bern in May of 1556. He did not go to Geneva with the Knox-Whittingham group. He became pastor of the church at Wesel, succeeding Miles Coverdale, but the Wesel church moved to Aarau. As pastor of the refugee church in Aarau, on 16 January 1559 he signed his congregation's acceptance of the Geneva church's appeal to maintain Reformed doctrine and practice upon their return to England. His license to leave Aarau was dated 11 January 1559, so he must have left for England soon after the middle of the month.[6]

Lever was soon preaching back in England, advising Elizabeth against using the title, "Supreme Head of the Church." He was appointed rector of Coventry and Archdeacon as well. In 1563, he became Master of Sherburn Hospital, Durham, and was promoted to the cathedral the next year. In 1567, he was deprived for nonconformity; he did not favor wearing ecclesiastical vestments, and repeatedly preached in London churches wearing his black academic gown. He had been a member of the Convocation of 1562–63 and subscribed to the articles for further reformation of the church.[7] His mastership at Sherburn Hospital, originally designated for lepers but later used primarily as a house for the poor, brought Lever into proximity with his erstwhile refugee cohort, William Whittingham. Whittingham had become Dean of Durham and Lever created a number of problems for him, eventually complaining to the Bishop of Durham, another erstwhile Geneva refugee, James Pilkington, that Whittingham was guilty of "works of impiety." Apparently the rift between Lever and Knox and those who sided with him ran deep, and Whittingham suffered the brunt of it in the 1560s. Lever had signed the letter the Cox party sent to Calvin justifying their stance against Knox and Whittingham, and the language used to depict Knox and his supporters was anything but complimentary.[8]

There is not a little irony here. Lever shared much with Whittingham, and the two of them could agree on a number of theological issues. Both were nonconformists, although Whittingham would later soften his position somewhat. In 1571, Lever was cited to appear before the Commission for his nonconformity, and in 1577, he was directed by the Bishop of Lichfield and Coventry, another fellow Geneva exile, Thomas Bentham, to suppress the prophesyings which he had encouraged in his archdeanery. He was not part of the classis movement which inspired the *First Admonition*.[9] Lever published *A Treatise on the right way from Danger of Sinne* from Geneva in 1556; later editions also appeared in 1571 and 1575.[10] Yet Lever did not represent the same ethos of the puritan group in Geneva. Moreover, his stay there did not parallel at any time the period of the Knox-Whittingham contingent, and he was never a member of the English Geneva church. Was he suspicious of the lack of loyalty to the motherland among the Knox-Whittingham contingent, and did the suspicion carry over when the exiles returned home? It would seem so, for the enigmatic Lever was rarely, if ever, associated with the radical puritans who undressed the nation in the *Admonition to Parliament* of 1572.

William Beauvoir was also mentioned as being in Geneva prior to 13 October 1555. He was likely a merchant, and was received as a resident of the city on 27 July 1556. He was appointed a deacon of the church in 1556, and remained such for the duration of his stay. His name appears as a signatory on the letter written by the Geneva exiles to their fellow exiles exhorting cooperation in the endeavor to keep the puritan concern alive upon their return to England; the letter was circulated when news of Mary's death reached Geneva.[11]

II. ORIGINAL MEMBERS OF THE GENEVA CHURCH

The following people came to Geneva 13 October 1555 to take advantage of the invitation of Calvin and the city of Geneva to establish a refugee English congregation. They were those who followed Whittingham from Frankfurt and became the backbone or nucleus of this noteworthy refugee community: **William** and **Jane Williams**; **Thomas** and **Anne Wood** with their daughter, **Deborah**; **Anthony** and **Elizabeth Gilby** with their son, **Goddred**; **William** and **Parnel Jackson** with their sons, **William** and **Andrew**, and their daughters, **Margery** and **Judith**; **John** and **Elene Holingham** with their son, **Daniel**; **Thomas** and **Johan Knolles**; **Christopher Goodman**; **William Whittingham**; **John Staunton**; **John Hilton**; **Christopher Seburne (als Plumer)**; **Richard Potter**; **John Ponce**; **John Maston**; and, **Thomas Crofton**.

William Williams seems to have been a life-long friend of Whittingham. He arrived with him at Frankfurt on 27 June 1554, and became the first Englishman to be given burgher status. He endorsed Whittingham's efforts to unite the two factions of English reformers at Frankfurt and, when matters turned sour, signed the secession letter of 27 August 1555. He became a resident of Geneva on 24 October and was received as a burgher.[12] Williams' main contribution seems to have been with money and emotional support for theologians such as Whittingham. In December of 1558, he collaborated with John Bodley and Rowland Hall to set up a printing press for the printing of tracts and other important religious writings. His influence and erudition in pastoral affairs were apparent by his annually being chosen an elder of the English church.

He stayed in Geneva with Whittingham and was one of the last refugees to leave on 30 May 1560. Collinson believes that Williams was Thomas Wood's brother-in-law, which would explain the close association of the two exiles in the records of events from 1554 to 1560. In fact, he became an elder, along with Wood, of the presbyterian London churches during the early 1570s, thereby carrying on the tradition he had learned firsthand at Geneva.[13]

Thomas Wood became a resident of Geneva on 24 October 1555, joining his brother-in-law, and signed himself as an exile from London. He had left England amidst the accusation that he was spreading a rumor that Edward was still alive, and arrived with Whittingham at Frankfurt on 27 June 1554.[14] His name appears abundantly in the *Troubles at Frankfurt*. He endorsed Whittingham's policies, shared in the invitation to the other English exiles to join the Frankfurt group, subscribed to the invitation to invite John Knox as preacher, opposed the Prayerbook, and announced his intention to secede from the Frankfurt congregation. Once in Geneva, Wood became an elder of the church, chosen by the congregation for the first time in 1557. Wood was a prolific writer of letters on behalf of various puritan causes in the 1560s. Collinson has shown that it was he, not Whittingham, who wrote the *Troubles at Frankfurt*.[15] He wrote this important piece of puritan propaganda in 1574 in the company of the radical presbyterian group which included John Field and Thomas Wilcox. As archivist and secretary to the London presbyterians, Wood had access to a number of important puritan documents. His letter to Whittingham in the same year as the composition of the *Troubles at Frankfurt* is telling, for he asked his former mentor for Calvin's letter in which the Genevan addressed the issue of the Second Edwardian Prayerbook. He was constantly in correspondence with fellow puritans and puritan supporters such as the Earls of Warwick, Huntington and Leicester.[16] In a letter from Knox to Anne Locke, Henry Locke's widow and also a Geneva exile, dated 2 September 1559, from St. Andrews, Knox mentioned that he had corresponded with Wood about the developments in Scotland and had asked Wood to spread the word to those in Geneva. Knox was especially concerned about Christopher Goodman, and was hopeful that both Goodman and Wood would pay him a visit in Scotland. Wood was named the godfather of Anthony Gilby's daughter, Ruthe, who was born (and later died) in Geneva. In 1574, Wood wrote to Gilby regarding his son-in-law, Ralph Hetherington, who was acting as a messenger between Wilcox and Gilby.[17]

In 1559, some London members of the Geneva group were hiding Goodman from the authorities, and Wood acted as their mediator with Geneva. In 1562, Wood was one of several disaffected Genevans who found at New Haven what Collinson calls "a cave of Adullum" where he and others practiced the Geneva pattern of worship. He preached to the army there along with Whittingham, William Kethe, Augustin Bradbridge and Jean Veron. It was probably Wood who was able to get these preaching posts for his cohorts due to his influence with the Earl of Warwick.[18] He returned to London sometime in 1563 to become the man of letters for the puritan cause.

During the vestment controversy of 1564–65, he appealed to the Earl of Huntington, petitioned the Earl of Leicester for Thomas Sampson and Goodman, and wrote to Cecil on 29 March 1566, after thirty-five London ministers had been suspended for nonconformity.

Robert Beaumont, a fellow Geneva exile, and then Vice-chancellor of Cambridge, was also indicted by Wood for applying the Advertisements, and the Earl of Leicester was charged with repressing prophesyings and condoning moral lapses as a consequence of such repression. The Earl of Warwick also received a letter from Wood in which the puritan urged him to continue to support puritan reforms.[19]

In 1571, Wood returned to his native Leicestershire where he purchased the lease of a manor house and demesne at Groby, not far from Ashby-de-la-Zouch where his former pastor, Gilby, lived. It was here that many of his letters were written. The letter to Whittingham in 1574, mentioned above, was significant for reasons in addition to Wood's request of Calvin's letter, for it indicates the true character of this puritan warrior. Whittingham had softened some of his puritan concerns, and it appeared to Wood that his friend and cohort of so many years, so many battles, had compromised what he had stood for in Frankfurt and Geneva. Wood chided him without embarrassment, and strongly urged him to return to his former zeal. The letter concluded with the note that many Genevan writings were being confiscated or burned, especially Beza's *Confessions* which had been translated by fellow Geneva exile, Robert Fills. Wood was afraid that the Geneva Bible might become a forbidden book, and if that were true, many other writings could very well face the same end.[20] Thomas Wood, an elder of the flock in Geneva, as well as of the London presbyterians, died a wealthy man in 1577. The executors of his will were Francis Hastings and Anthony Gilby.

Anthony Gilby was one of the most important of the Geneva exiles. He was born in 1510 in Lincolnshire, educated at Christ's College, Cambridge, from which he received the M.A. in 1535. He was well schooled in biblical and classical languages which prepared him to assist in no small way in the compilation of the Geneva Bible of 1560. He possibly studied at Basel in 1555, but earlier appeared in Frankfurt during the squabbles of 1554, where he tried to mediate between the Knox and Cox factions.[21] He eventually sided with Knox and Whittingham, and came with the latter to Geneva on 13 October 1555. He was immediately elected as one of the ministers of the English church, and later in exile he served also as an elder. Gilby helped to send a letter to the Frankfurt refugee congregation which was designed to soften the charge of schism leveled at the Whittingham party. Although he defended Knox and those who supported him at Frankfurt, he appeared to communicate effectively and listen openly to counter positions in order to promote unity.[22]

While in Geneva, Gilby was a busy person. He not only assisted in the translation and annotation of the 1560 edition of the Bible, but he also helped to formulate the Genevan church order of 1556. His pastoral and ministerial concerns were widely apparent. He may have been the mind and hand behind the circular letter sent by the Geneva exiles on 15 December 1558 to their fellow exiles on the Continent; the letter affirmed the necessity of uniformity in Reformed theology and practice in the anticipation of returning to England under Elizabeth I. He remained in Geneva as one of the last of the refugees to leave, returning home sometime in 1560.[23]

Gilby wrote one theological treatise while in Geneva. In 1556, his *Treatise on Election* appeared. In the treatise, he mentioned that he had fashioned a commentary on Malachi "three years ago" in which he adumbrated the doctrine of predestination. He subsequently published several other editions of the *Treatise on Election* including one added to a republication of *A briefe Declaration of the chiefe Poyntes of Christian Religion, set foorth in a Table made by Theodore Beza,* which had been translated by Whittingham in 1556. Gilby thought that Beza had argued the "chief ground of this doctrine," and that the principal points thereof "are so deeply opened" that there seemed to "want nothing that was possible in so few lines to be uttered...."[24] Yet Gilby seemed pleased enough to see his treatise published.

This book, however, was not his first literary effort. In 1547, Gilby had answered Stephen Gardiner's vindication of the doctrine of transubstantiation in *An Answer to the devilish detection of Stephane Gardiner, Bishoppe of Winchester.*[25] Gilby believed that Bucer, Oecolampadius and John Frith had adequately remonstrated the notion of transubstantiation, including quotations and references from the scriptures and the church fathers, "if these men would suffer their books to come to light."[26] But Gilby was compelled to respond to Gardiner with his own arguments. In addition, in 1551, Gilby had written a commentary on the prophet Micah; it was published from London, and contained almost identical characteristics in the treatment of the text and the preface Gilby appended to the work that one finds in the 1560 edition of the Geneva Bible. For example, Micah was considered a "diligent watchman," warning Israel of the impending judgment "that the Lord himself will come down most terribly to the wicked and the mountains shall melt, the valleys shall vade [fade] and vanish like wax before the firey flame."[27]

This "Deuteronomic view of history"[28] so prevalent in Gilby's Commentary on Micah was to reappear in 1554 in his preface to Knox's *A Faythfull admonition* entitled, *The Epistle of a Banyished Manne out of Leycester Shire, sometyme one of the Preachers of*

Goddes Worde there. In 1558, from Geneva, Gilby again wrote a preface to a treatise by Knox. The title of Knox's work was *The Appellation from the Sentence Pronounced by the Bishops and Clergy,* and Gilby's preface bore the title, *An Admonition to England and Scotland, to call them to Repentance.* As might be expected, the heart of Gilby's long preface was the condemnation of England's apostasy and the pronouncement of God's judgment unless she repented and reformed her ways. In these writings, Gilby was convinced that Mary Tudor's succession to the throne was part of divine judgment upon the commonwealth, for "doth not Esaias reckon this also as the extremity of all plagues for the wickedness of the people, to have 'women raised up to rule over you'?"[29] The rule of Mary had seen the rise of Jezebel and the prophets of Baal. Echoing Jesus' Parable of the Vineyard, Gilby saw the vineyard as God's granting to England the prepared soil of reformation, and England had responded with laborers in the persons of the reformers. Alas, even the faithful laborers were being stoned and killed. All that remained was for the true son to descend upon the nation and be subjected to persecution and martyrdom by wicked and cruel tyrants!

> For this I admonish you, O ye people of England, wheresoever you bescattered or placed, that unless ye do right speedily repent of your former negligence, it is not the Spaniards only that ye have to fear as rods of Gods wrath, but all other nations, France, Turkey, and Denmark, yea, all creatures shall be armed against you for the contempt of those times when your heavenly Father so mercifully called you. To what contempt was Gods word, and the admonition of his Prophets, come in all estates before God did strike, men are not now ignorant.[30]

Thus in playing the role of a sixteenth-century prophet deeply imbibed in a Deuteronomic theory of retribution, calling for England's repentance and return to the "true religion" of the Reformation, Gilby reflected a tradition which he inherited from English Reformers as early as William Tyndale.[31]

Gilby's return to England changed the thrust of his theological interests. He discovered, to his chagrin, that Elizabeth was attempting to thwart a more thorough-going reformation by retaining a great many "popish remnants" from Mary's reign. His main concern was the use of vestments, caps and surplices. But there were other concerns—the lack of Bible reading and preaching, the idolatrous administration of the Lord's Supper, and the total lack of ecclesiastical discipline and order in the churches. Two letters addressed to his former colleagues in exile can be found in a little book entitled, *Tracts Concerning Vestments,* preceded by the following frontispiece: *To my louynge brethren that is troublyed abowt the popist aparrell, two short and Comfortable Epistels.* The letters were probably written prior to 1566. His main objection to the wearing of vestments, which he called "popish rags," was the hypocrisy of wearing a white vestment for special, religious occasions, and a black one for non-religious occasions. The true mark of the minister was not the color or type of gown he wore, but the feeding of the flock of God, and the worst impropriety was that people were not being edified. Vestments added nothing to edification, and what was more to the point, they had no apostolic precedent.[32]

In 1570, Gilby compiled all of his objections to such abuses in *A View of Antichrist,* "a clear glass wherein may be seen the dangerous and desperate diseases of our English Church." In this work Archbishop Matthew Parker, dubbed "the Pope of Lambeth," came under special attack for perpetuating the Queen's desire to have a clergy who looked the part. Even if St. Paul were revivified and came back to preach in England, the Archbishop would not allow him to mount a pulpit until he first subscribed to the wearing of the "popish corned cape, surplice, cap, and such like idolatrous stuff."[33] There would never be a reformation as long as prelates such as Parker allowed a little poison to contaminate the whole pottage by acquiescing to the Pope and Romish ceremonies.[34] Parker attempted to hold Gilby to wearing ecclesiastical vestments, and referred the Genevan's non-compliance to Bishop Grindal of York. But Grindal was helpless to do much about Gilby's resistance, and his case was referred to the commissioners in the south.[35]

The crowning effort of this polemic was, of course, the famous *An Admonition to Parliament,* written by several puritans in 1572. Usually attributed to John Field and Thomas Wilcox, the *Admonition* could not have been written without the inspiration and input of Gilby.[36] After Parliament met in 1571, the authors of the *Admonition* were compelled to add several additional points to their list of grievances:

> We strive for a true religion and government of the church, and shew you the right way to throw out Antichrist both head and tail, and that we will not so much as communicate with the tail of the beast: but they after they have thrust Antichrist out by the head, go about to pull him in again by the tail, cunningly coloring it, lest any man should espie his footsteps....[37]

Gilby continued his puritan polemic in 1579 when he published *A Preface to An Answer made by Oliver Carter...unto certaine Popish Questions and Demandes,* and again in 1581 with *A Pleasavnt*

Dialogve, Betweene a Souldior of Barwicke, and an English Chaplaine, the latter called by Collinson "an early puritan exercise in the art of 'pleasant' badinage which would one day give birth to Martin Marprelate."[38] The entertaining piece feigned a dialogue between a soldier and an English cleric, a former soldier himself, "who had gotten a pluralitie of benefices, and yet had but one eye, and no learning...but...was priestly appareled in all points." He obviously had become one of Elizabeth's ministers who had compromised what the puritans believed was a true reformation of religion. Now that Parliament had not taken heed to the puritan "First Admonition" all hope was lost, and "we must turn to God by prayer, and that which we can do by words and by writing." "And I do think assuredly," the soldier told his captain-cleric, "that God doth call us all by this controversy, to a reckoning, for our cold and careless trifling in Religion: by the which Atheism, Papism, and Lutheranism strive against us faint soldiers, hoping for victory."[39]

Gilby had written *A Pleasavnt Dialogve* seven years before the piece was published, and the vestment controversy was still raging in his mind. It is clear that the soldier, named Miles Monopodios, expressed Gilby's ongoing impatience with the Elizabethan Settlement because of its association with Roman Catholicism. Throughout the satire there is a running reference to "Genevians" who challenged Elizabeth and her bishops by making a stand against the idolatry of vestments. The priest, given the name Sir Bernard Blynkard by Gilby, had little good to say about the "Genevians" and their religiosity— they "have nothing in the church but naked walls, and a poor fellow in a bare gown, telling a long take [tale], and brawling and chiding with all his authority." The priest even chides them for their woeful proximity to Anabaptism, but Miles comes to the defense of the "Genevians" and the London ministers who were attempting to implement the goals and aspirations of the Genevan church. They were clearly not Anabaptists![40]

But the priest strikes at the Achilles' heel of the puritan defense against Anabaptism by accusing them of failure to obey the civil magistrate, thus sharing in Anabaptist heresy. The soldier retorts that the doctrine of obedience to civil rulers, granted a biblical notion, "doth bind us in conscience, to have a love and reverence unto our Prince, as unto Gods Lieuetenaunt" and that we should do all we can to support the office of the magistrate, but only so long as right order is maintained and evil and wickedness are punished. If God's people are required by the magistrate to do evil, the choice to obey God rather than man is the only conscionable response. If the government fosters evil and wrongdoing, the faithful may even share in wrongdoing by praying for the magistrate, "for we must abstain from all show of evil." Miles was convinced that God's plagues were falling upon the nation for not rooting out idolatry. Some of the "chief gospellers" were being thrown in prison, "one spoileth another of liberty and living, and the papists live quietly indeed, and laugh in their sleeves."[41] Miles then puts together a prodigious list of arguments, complete with major and minor premises, to bolster his position against vestments. Each major and minor premise is vouchsafed by scriptural citations and copious references to Martin Bucer. We have heard the arguments before: vestments do not edify, they are precepts of human invention and cannot be corroborated by apostolic example, they give offense to those who cannot abide them, etc. As the dialogue draws to a conclusion, the priest must assume Gilby's caricature; he is unlearned, drunk with wealth and power, ignorant of preaching and the Word of God, oblivious to a spiritual warfare raging around him, and in a state of lamentable dogmatic confusion. The piece ends with "An hundred pointes of Poperie, yet remayning, which deforme the Englishe reformation," identical to the table found in Gilby's *View of Antichrist.*[42]

In the later stages of his career, Gilby translated works of his erstwhile Genevan mentors, Calvin and Beza. In 1570, he translated *Commentaries of that diuine Iohn Calvine, vpon the Prophet Daniell,* and dedicated the work to his patron, the Earl of Huntington. In the preface, Gilby referred to himself as "one of Calvin's scholars," a fact for which he praised God "more than for any earthly matter." He had decided to translate only the first six chapters of Calvin's commentary because they seemed worthwhile to his present situation "which do treat of the particular histories wrought by God in his time."[43]

In 1581, *The Psalms of Dauid, trvly Opened and explained by Paraphrasis* appeared, printed by Henry Denham. This work was originally written in Latin by Theodore Beza and was translated by Gilby. It was dedicated to "The Right Honorable and Virtuous Lady, the Lady Katherine, Countess of Huntington," and echoed many of Gilby's past concerns. He was especially concerned that during the last twenty-two years "the horrible sins of former times are not yet purged with true tears of repentance." Many idolatrous ways still persisted, "especially in kneeling down and worshipping that wafer cake, the vilest and weakest idol that ever was imagined upon the earth." He believed that this little book of psalms and prayers could help to bring England to repentance. He was convinced "that certain plagues" hang presently over England for the sins of Mary's reign which yet could be discerned. His love for his country and admiration for Beza caused him to engage in the translation of this piece. Every congregation needs a pastor who can give clear meaning to the Psalms. As with his other biblical writings, a very decided Deuteronomic motif is apparent.[44] England had her own "Jehosaphat." Elizabeth could now follow the example of Israel's rulers who tore down every form of idolatry to establish God's true religion. The "book of the Lord" should be rediscovered, as it was in the time of Josiah, so that it may become the hub of the whole church, her worship, discipline and doctrine. Elizabeth should send forth her princes and ministers, and give them the book of the Lord. Then the fear of the Lord would come upon every city and country, "that they shall not make war against our Jehosophat...."[45]

Christopher Goodman was an Oxford graduate, having finished his M.A. in 1544 and his B.D. in 1551. He had been appointed Lady Margaret Professor of Divinity in 1548. He became an exile during Mary's reign, first seen at Strasburg where he felt the familiar mentoring of Peter Martyr; his name appears on the list of signatories of the letter sent from Strasburg to the English congregation at Frankfurt. He spent the winter of 1554–55 at Basel, but eventually made his way to Frankfurt. He sided with the Knox-Whittingham party and was part of the original company of English refugees to settle in Geneva, arriving with Whittingham and the others on 15 October 1555. He was appointed one of two ministers; Gilby had also been appointed to take the place of Knox until he returned from Scotland.[46]

It was one of Goodman's sermons that prompted him to write the controversial *How Svperior Powers Oght to be Obeyd* in 1558. One of the elders in the Geneva church, Whittingham, had written a preface to the tract assuring the reader that Goodman's book had the approval of "the best learned in these parts" and that the author had checked out his major argument with such notable persons.[47] In a letter written to Peter Martyr from Geneva on 20 August 1558, Goodman reported that he had discussed the contents of his book with Calvin, even before it was published, and that Calvin deemed some of his propositions "somewhat harsh," especially to "those who are in the place of power, and that for this reason they should be handled with caution." Nevertheless, Calvin was in basic agreement.[48] Both Calvin and Beza, however, denied that they had known about Goodman's treatise until after it was published. In a letter to Lord Bacon in 1559, Matthew Parker wrote of Goodman's treatise,

if such principles be spread into men's heads, as now they be framed, and referred to the judgment of the subject to discuss what is tyranny, and to discern whether his prince, his landlord, his master, is a tyrant, by his own fancy and collection supposed; what Lord of the council shall ride quietly minded in the streets among desperate beasts? What minister shall be sure in his bed chamber?[49]

John Jewell informed Peter Martyr from London in the spring of 1559 that he had heard that Goodman was in England, but "he dare not show his face."[50]

Goodman's treatise advocated rebellion, civil resistance and even tyrannicide. Elizabeth's awareness of the book made her understandably angry, and her subsequent enmity was at once directed at Goodman, but also at the whole Geneva community—the exiles and the entire city. Beza wrote in 1566 to Bullinger,

> For as to our Church, I would have you know that it is so hateful to the Queen of England, that on this account she never said a single word in acknowledgment of the gift of my Annotations. The reason for her dislike is twofold; one, because we are accounted too severe and precise..., the other is, because formerly, though without my knowledge, during the lifetime of Queen Mary, two books were published in the English language, one by Master Knox against the Government of Women, the other by Master Goodman on the Rights of the Magistrates. As soon as we learned the contents of each we were much displeased, and their sale was forbidden in consequence; but she, nothwithstanding, cherishes the opinion she had taken into her head.[51]

In June of 1559, Knox had begged Goodman to join him in Edinburgh. One of the reasons for Knox's keen interest in Goodman, although he admitted that he loved Goodman as much as his own flesh and blood, was that Knox's family was traveling under Goodman's care since the time they had left Geneva. Goodman apparently went to Scotland in the fall of that year, for in October he was made a member of the Scottish council, and in November he became minister at Ayr. He held several additional posts, including preacher at St. Andrews and the Isle of Man, until the winter of 1565. From Scotland, Goodman assured Calvin that England was mired in all sorts of ungodliness, avarice and greed, inevitable results of female government.[52]

Although the Earl of Warwick had tried to get him back into England as early as 1562, Goodman ventured back only in 1565. He became chaplain to Sir Henry Sidney and in 1570 he was appointed a living at Alford, New Chester and made Archdeacon of Richmond. He was relieved of his duties because of nonconformity, and he appears to have been in London at the time of the 1571 Parliament with a living in Bedfordshire from May until the following March.[53] Clearly a marked person, Goodman was summoned before the Lambeth

Commission. The commission would not hear of compromises desired by puritans in order to preach, and Goodman's trail was hounded by the Queen's authorities. Finally, in 1571, Goodman was forced to make two, perhaps three concessions. He was asked to sign a retraction of the excesses in his book, and openly avow female government. He confessed that he would daily pray for the Queen's government, and admitted that he never intended that Mary should have been assassinated by civil disobedience. He promised never to write or teach these matters again, expressing hope that he might be given a "favorable allowance" so that he could continue preaching. These recantations seem to have occurred on 23 April 1571. An additional statement was extracted from Goodman on 26 April which expressly affirmed allegiance to Elizabeth as "my only liege lady and most lawful queen and sovereign," as well as a retraction of his position on the right of women to rule. He signed the recantation on 29 May 1571.[54]

During John Field's confinement in 1571, Goodman acted as publisher of Cartwright's *Replye* to Whitgift's *Answere to the Admonition*, and he probably had a hand in writing the *Second Admonition to Parliament.* He complained to the Earl of Leicester that he was "beaten with three rods" (doubtless his recantation and retractions) and forbidden to preach.[55] In August of 1571, he appears to have returned to Chester where not much is known of his activities until the 1580s. His leadership was evident in the monthly exercises or prophesyings, then prohibited in the south, which were set up in "the middle town of every several deanery." He is known to have preached a controversial sermon at Exeter in 1583.[56] Whitgift could not silence or repress his efforts in the puritan cause. It seems that the Archbishop lived under the ominous cloud of fear that Goodman's book was being reprinted; that had been Parker's fear as well.

William Whittingham was clearly the leader of the English church in Geneva. It was really he who was responsible for the decision to leave Frankfurt in search of a new church-home, and his conversations with Calvin resulted in the Knox-Whittingham faction moving to Geneva. Before his exile, he had studied at Oxford; he became senior student at Christ's Church in 1547, and graduated M.A. in February of 1548. He was granted leave to travel on the Continent during Edward's reign; he spent most of his time in France at the University of Orleans, although he also visited Geneva and traveled briefly in Germany. He returned to England in May of 1553.[57] As an acquaintance of Peter Martyr, Whittingham was instrumental in getting Martyr to London where the latter supported Cranmer's reforms of the mass. When Mary ascended to the throne, Whittingham used his influence to appeal in behalf of Martyr, asking for an honorable passport from England to the Continent with "permission to remove all his goods."[58] Whittingham left for Germany and arrived in Frankfurt on 27 June 1554. After the troubles at Frankfurt, he came to Geneva on 13 October 1555 to begin a new experiment in the restoration of apostolic Christian polity, discipline and doctrine.

During his sojourn in Geneva (and no other English refugee spent more time there than Whittingham) he married Katherine Jaquemayne. Two children were recorded baptized in the *Livre des Anglois*. He was elected an elder of the church on several occasions, a deacon once, but never a minister. He would serve as minister, however, during Elizabeth's reign; this became a matter of no little consternation, and Whittingham would appeal to his having been ordained a minister at the encouragement, and probably the installation, of Calvin in 1559.[59] Whittingham was a Bible scholar and Christian humanist. In 1557, John Bodley published from Geneva Whittingham's New Testament with annotations. It was his inspiration which produced the complete Bible of 1560 with fuller annotations as well as other literary paraphernalia. It was published in Geneva in May of 1560, and Whittingham, with a few of his fellow refugees, remained in Geneva until it was finished. He also turned many psalms into metre; seven of these were included among the fifty-one psalms published in 1556 as part of the servicebook which Whittingham had already drawn up in Frankfurt. Others were revisions of Sternhold. Whittingham was also responsible for a metrical version of the Ten Commandments which was appended to the servicebook. His eminence as a Hebraist allowed him to contribute more to the formation of the liturgy of the English church at Geneva than any of the exiles.[60] His other literary activities in Geneva consisted of writing prefaces to tracts by Nicholas Ridley on the Lord's Supper and by Goodman on the right of resistance, and translating Beza's treatise on predestination in 1556.[61]

Whittingham's return to England was initially characterized by travel. He accompanied the Earl of Bedford on his mission to the court of France. Later, he went with the Earl of Warwick in the latter's defense of Newhaven against the French, where he became preacher to the military forces, and where, it is important to recall, a church order was devised by like-minded puritans to emulate the Genevan pattern without deference to the Prayerbook. He gained a high opinion from the Earl and it was probably due to his influence and similar plaudits from Cecil, that Whittingham became Dean of Durham. He supported the London "Strangers' Churches" with money, and was known to have celebrated communion with the

French congregation in London. Whittingham preached before the Queen on 2 September 1563, and wrote to the Earl of Leicester in 1564 concerning the vestments to which he was strenuously opposed. Two years later he addressed the same letter, minus the personal references to the Earl, to "my faythful Brethren now afflycted...." The letters were characteristically puritan of the more radical sort, and indicate that Whittingham was still a source of inspiration and exemplification of the Genevan model of piety and theology.[62]

Within the next decade, however, Whittingham seems to have changed. His fellow refugee and stalwart in the puritan cause, Thomas Wood, thought that when Cecil became Lord Treasurer, Whittingham changed his position on the wearing of ecclesiastical vestments, and that his rationale was the caveat of Calvin that the ministry of the church should not go unheeded or prohibited by external adiaphora. It was doubtless this change which caused him to be the recipient of hard, chiding letters from some of the erstwhile Genevans.[63] They had become truly confused about Whittingham's position. Whittingham had refused to abide by the requirements to wear the surplice and the use of the Prayerbook in March of 1564. Several months before, he addressed a letter to Cecil, on 19 December 1563, in which he explained Durham's response to Parker's "An Office of Prayer and Fasting for the plague and other judgments" which Cecil had convinced the Queen to bind also on the province of York. Whittingham's response is a good example of the addition of the puritan emphasis on preaching in the context of carrying out the Queen's wishes for prayer and fasting.[64]

Perhaps it was in 1569 that Whittingham began thinking about the change. The question of how candid his efforts were in adhering to the desires of Elizabeth's via media was complicated by his ordination or the perceived lack thereof. Events began to stir when Thomas Lever, one-time fellow Genevan exile and then Master of Sherburn House, a hospital near Durham, complained to James Pilkington, the Bishop of Durham and also fellow Genevan exile, about some of the "works of impiety" in Durham. Rumor had it that several stone coffins, having belonged to the priors, had been dug up and used as troughs for horses and swine, and that the covers were then being used to cover the Dean's own house. Additional iconoclasm was charged against the Dean's leadership, the long and short of which was to accuse Whittingham of unnecessary anti-monastic fervor and license.[65]

Bishop Pilkington had stronger ties to Whittingham than Lever, and was quite aware of the hard feelings between Lever and the Knox-Whittingham group which were made evident at Frankfurt. Our sources are not adequate to fill in the necessary, intriguing details, and exactly why Whittingham became the brunt of Lever's accusations remains somewhat oblique. Pilkington, who had supported Whittingham, died in 1576. It was about this time that an official commission was sent to investigate the charges against Whittingham; Edwin Sandys, Archbishop of York, was dispatched by the Queen to head the commission. What happened at this juncture is not clear. Strype reports that the Archbishop was refused the visitation which led him naturally to conclude that Durham was not implementing the prescribed orders, and that only excommunication, a matter out of his hands, could undo the mess which Whittingham had helped to create.[66]

This episode, the veracity of which must remain in doubt, corroborates nevertheless the reputation that Whittingham had as a radical puritan and nonconformist during the decades of the 1560s and 1570s. In 1571, for example, the Queen pressed hard for uniformity, and several puritans, including Gilby, Thomas Sampson and Whittingham, were targeted for nonconformity. Whittingham was asked to appear before the commission at Lambeth by 31 August of that year; whether he did or not is not known, but he seemed to have left the impression that it was his intention to do so.[67]

It was in the late 1570s, however, that the unresolved problems in Durham forced Elizabeth to appoint yet another commission. In 1578, a commission was sent specifically to investigate the cathedral church and Whittingham's papers of ordination. The commission subsequently became divided over its findings, for one member reported that Whittingham was not suitably ordained, while the president of the commission was sympathetic to the informal kind of ordination which Whittingham had received from Calvin in 1559. Whittingham brought forward two certificates of ordination, one signed by eight persons, dated 8 July 1578, which proved his ordination "by lot and election." Archbishop Sandys remonstrated that this was to no effect in the Church of England. Whittingham countered with citations from Calvin "who affirmeth, that the election was not, nor is to be drawn into example." Apparently a month later, Whittingham presented a notary-sworn certificate, signed by eight persons, with changes advocated by the commission. The final report of the chancellor, however, invalidated Whittingham's ordination, something Elizabeth wanted all along, on the ground that, among other objections, no "*externae solemnitates, authontatem ordinantis*" were signatories to the certificate. John Bodley was the only name approved by the commission; Bodley had been with Whittingham in Geneva.[68]

The matter was further complicated by the president of the commission who expressed sympathy for Whittingham's case. In his report, he avowed that he would accept the Genevan ordination if only for the pragmatic reason that all ordinations in Continental Reformed churches would thereby not be called into scrutiny by the English! Furthermore, he argued, the commission had not been unanimous in its rendering, particularly because of the adamant disagreements between Sandys, Archbishop of York, and the Dean of York, who sympathized with Whittingham. We have only John Strype's uneven account of the Durham affair, beginning in 1569 and concluding with the visitation of 1578, and he was not sure how the matter ended. Whittingham, alas, was to die six months later.

Whittingham's career was somewhat of an enigma. It is said that he loved music and the arts, "allowing singing in the church" and being careful to provide the best songs and anthems "that could be got out of the queen's chapel to furnish his choir with."[69] Yet the events at the Cathedral of Durham during his deanship might seem overly bizarre in their iconoclasm, for by the end of his office in 1579, little remained of the traditional furnishings of the cathedral except those austere items which could provide morning and evening prayer, the communion and sermons.[70]

Was this a reflection of his Genevan experience? To a degree, it was. What is more, however, is that it is a reflection of the radical kind of puritan ethos the Genevan exiles represented when they returned to Elizabeth's via media only to discover that the Church of England was far removed from primitive, apostolic Christianity which they recollected to have been so bountiful in Geneva.

The remaining names of those who arrived in Geneva on 13 October 1555 are not well known. **John Staunton** was from Nottingham, and had been in Frankfurt with Whittingham as early as 29 July 1554. He subscribed to the invitation to Knox to serve as minister, as well as to the letter sent to the Strasburg church, via Grindal and Chambers, concerning opposition to the Prayerbook. He was granted residence in Geneva on 24 October, and was chosen deacon of the English church in both 1555 and 1566.[71] **Christopher Seburne,** alias "Plummer," was made a resident also on 24 October and was appointed deacon with Staunton. Garrett is of the opinion that he was from the Seborne family of Gloucestershire and Herefordshire; the family had played a role in the Welsh march during the reign of Mary.[72] **John Ponce** has been identified erroneously as John Ponet.[73] Council minutes of Strasburg indicate that Ponet was in Strasburg at this time. This Ponce was probably John Poyntz, fourth son of Sir Nicholas Poyntz of Iron Acton, Gloucestershire. Sir

Nicholas had been a supporter of Lady Jane Grey and defended the Wyatt rebellion. John is named in his father's will.[74]

NOTES

[1]Mitchell, *Livre des Anglois*, p. 5. Peter Lorimer believes that most of the entries were in Knox's handwriting. See Lorimer, *John Knox and the Church of England* (London: H. S. King, 1875), pp. 201ff.

[2]Mitchell, p. 5. The *Livre des Anglois* may be found also in J. Southerden Burn, *History of Parish Registers,* Laing's edition of Knox's *Works* (New York: AMS, 1966), Horatio B. Hackett, "Church-Book of the Puritans at Geneva, from 1555 to 1560," *Bibliotheca Sacra* (1892), 469ff, and Th. Heyer, "Notice sur la Colonie Anglais, Ètablie à Genève de 1555 à 1560," *Memoires et Documents, publiés par la Sociétié d'archéologie de Genèva* IX (1855), 337–68. The first two parts will also be found in Lorimer, *ibid.*

[3]See, e.g., Dan G. Danner, "Anthony Gilby: Puritan in Exile—A Biographical Approach," *Church History* 40 (1971), 412–22; see also my "Christopher Goodman and the English Protestant Tradition of Civil Disobedience," *Sixteenth Century Journal* 8 (1977), 61–73, and "Calvin and Puritanism: The Career of William Whittingham," *Calviniana. Ideas and Influence of Jean Calvin*, Robert V. Schnucker ed., *Sixteenth Century Essays & Studies* X (1988), 151–63.

[4]Garrett, *Marian Exiles*, pp. 295–96.

[5]See the helpful biographical treatment of Lever in *English Reprints*, V.xii, *Sermons of Thomas Lever*, ed. Edward Arber (London: 1870), pp. 3–8.

[6]Garrett, pp. 219–21.

[7]Sidney Lee, *Dictionary of National Biography* , ed. Leslie Stephen (New York: Macmillan, 1908), XI, 1021–22 (hereafter cited *DNB*). On the Convocation of 1562, see Patrick Collinson, *Elizabethan Puritan Movement* (Berkeley: University of California Press, 1967), pp. 65ff., and William A. Haugaard, *Elizabeth and the English Reformation* (Cambridge: University Press, 1968), pp. 333–40, *passim*.

[8]See John Strype, *Annals of the Reformation* (Oxford: Clarendon Press, 1824), II.ii, 107–09.

[9]*English Reprints,* pp. 3–8.

[10]See Collinson, *Elizabethan Puritan Movement,* p. 118. Cf. *A Treatise on the right way from Danger of Sinne & vengeance in this wicked world, vnto godly wealth and saluation in christe.* Made by Th. Leuer, and now newly augmented. Printed by Henrie Bynneman for George Byshop (London, 1575).

[11]Garrett, pp. 83–84; *Troubles,* p. 188. Cf. Martin, p. 256, and Mitchell, p. 7.

[12]Garrett, pp. 335–36.

[13]Collinson, "The Authorship of *A Brieff Discours off the Troubles...*," *Journal of Ecclesiastical History* 9 (1958), 188–208, and *Letters of Thomas Wood*, ed. Patrick Collinson (London: University/Athone Press, 1960), pp. 7–8; cf. Collinson, *Elizabethan Puritan Movement,* p. 133. Note should be made of Mitchell's earlier identification of Williams as Wood's brother-in-law in his

footnotes to the *Livre des Anglois,* p. 1. Collinson had originally identified Williams as the father-in-law of Wood before he came to Mitchell's same conclusion.

[14]Garrett, p. 343. This was Garrett's conjecture based on the possible linkage of Wood with the Thomas Wood who was mercer of London and servant of Henry Locke. Locke had been stationed at Antwerp and Garrett surmises that Wood and Whittingham may have stayed with him while negotiating with the Frankfurt magistrates. Collinson, "The Authorship of *A Brieff Discours off the Troubles...,*" is doubtful that any genuine link between the two Woods can be made, but cf. *Godly People,* pp. 50ff, 278–79.

[15]*Journal of Ecclesiastical History* 9 (1958), 188–208.

[16]Collinson, *Godly People,* pp. 53–73. Cambridge University Library Mss., Mm. 1.43, p. 439; Laing, *Works of John Knox,* VI, Part I, 78–79.

[17]Collinson, "The Authorship of *A Brief Discours off the Troubles...."*

[18]*Ibid.*

[19]*Ibid.*

[20]*Ibid.*

[21]John and J. A. Venn, *Alumni catabrigienses* (Cambridge: University Press, 1922), Part I, Vol. II, 215. Garrett does not consider it likely that Gilby was enrolled as a student in Basel; see Garrett, pp. 161–62.

[22]Mitchell, p. 12.

[23]Benjamin Brook, *The Lives of the Puritans* (London: James Black, 1813), I, 278–84; E. T. Bradley, *DNB,* VII, 1218–19.

[24]Anthony Gilby, *A Briefe Treatise of Election and Reprobation, with certen answers to the obiections of the aduersaries of thys doctrine* (Geneva, 1556), fo. Aii, r.

[25]Gardiner's treatise was entitled, *A Detection of the Devil's Sophistrie, wherewith he robbeth the unlearned people of the true belief, in the most blessed Sacrament of the aulter* (1546).

[26]Gilby, *An Answer...,* fo. ix, r.

[27]Anthony Gilby, *A Commentarye upon the Prophet Mycah* (London, 1551), fo. Aii, v.

[28]I originally heard this phrase in reference to the English Reformation from James C. Spalding. The reference is to the Deuteronomist or D-source of the documentary hypothesis which postulates multiple authorship of the Pentateuch. The Deuteronomist was a revisionist who reworked historical materials in light of the theory of covenant and retributive justice. English reformers such as Gilby looked in retrospect at England's past to judge whether God had either blessed or cursed his new Israel. Thus England, as the new Israel of God covenanted with him for a reformation of religion, was the domain of his on-going activity in history, and his retributive justice was thereby interpreted according to successes and failures of the English Reformation as defined by these divines. See James C. Spalding, "Restitution as a Normative Factor for Puritan Dissent,

Journal of the American Academy of Religion 44 (1976), 47–63. Cf. Richard L. Greaves, "John Knox and the Covenant Tradition," *Journal of Ecclesiastical History* 24 (1973), 23–32; Michael McGiffert, "Covenant, Crown, and Commons in Elizabethan Puritanism," *Journal of British Studies* 20 (1980), 32–52; and, Theodore Dwight Bozeman, "Federal Theology and the 'National Covenant': An Elizabethan Presbyterian Case Study," *Church History* 61 (1992), 394–407. The term "federal theology" is often used to depict the same sentiment (Bozeman prefers "Israelite paradigm"); it was not strictly the covenant of works that one finds in Bullinger's (or Zwingli's) theology.

[29]Laing, *Works of John Knox*, IV, 554.

[30]*Ibid.*, IV, 565.

[31]See William Tyndale's *Five Books of Moses called the Pentateuch, being a verbatim reprint of the edition of 1530* (Carbondale: Southern Illinois University Press, 1967), and Tyndale's *The Prophet Jonas with an introduccion before teachinge to understand him* (Antwerp, 1531?). Cf. Michael McGiffert, "William Tyndale's Conception of Covenant," *Journal of Ecclesiastical History* 32 (1981), 167–84.

[32] Anthony Gilby, *Tracts Concerning Vestments* (no colophon or date), fo. Ciii, v.

[33]*Parte of a register, contayninge sundrie matters, written by diuers godly and learned in our time, which stand for, and desire the reformation of our church, in Discipline and ceremonies, according to the pure worde of God, and the Lawe of our Lande* (London, 1593), fo. H1, v.

[34]*Ibid.*, fos. H4, v–L1, r.

[35]Brook, I, 278–84; John Strype, *The Life and Acts of Edmund Grindal* (Oxford: Clarendon Press, 1821), pp. 252–53. See Collinson, *Godly People,* pp. 36ff, 344.

[36]Evidence of Gilby's involvement in the events which led to the *First Admonition* and the furor it caused in its wake can be shown in Letters to Gilby, Thomas Baker Mss. Vol. 32, Mm. 1.43, pp. 426–48. See also Danner, "Anthony Gilby...," *Church History* 40 (1971), 412–21.

[37]*An Admonition to Parliament* (London, 1572), fos. Biii, v–Bv, r.

[38]Collinson, *Elizabethan Puritan Movement,* p. 78.

[39]Anthony Gilby, *A Pleasavnt Dialogve...* (no colophon, 1581), fo. A8, r.

[40]*Ibid.*, fos. C8, v–D3, v.

[41]*Ibid.,* fo. E4, v.

[42]*Ibid.*, fos. N3, r–N4, r.

[43]*Commentaries of that diuine Iohn Caluine, vpon the Prophet Daniell...* (London: John Day, 1570).

[44]*Psalms of Dauid Trvly Opened and explaned by Paraphrasis...* (Henry Denham, 1581), fo. A3, v.

[45]*View of Antichrist,* fo. I4, v.

[46]*Troubles,* p. 23; Garrett, pp. 162–64. Garrett points out that prior to his exile, Goodman was in the company of conspirators Bartlett Green and William Thomas, both known to have plotted Mary Tudor's death. Cf. N. D. [Robert Parsons], *The Third Part of a Treatise Intitled: of three Conversions of England: conteyninge...The First Six Months* (1604), pp. 220ff.

[47]Christopher Goodman, *How Svperior Powers Oght to be Obeyd...* (Geneva, 1558), fos. Aii, v–Aiii, r.

[48]*Zurich Letters,* III, 771.

[49]John Strype, *The Life and Acts of Matthew Parker* (Oxford: Clarendon Press, 1821), III, 85.

[50]The letter was dated 28 April 1559; *Zurich Letters*, III, 21. On 2 September 1559, Knox wrote to Anne Locke that Goodman had come to the border of England and had since returned, "but I cannot understand whether my brother is repaired." Laing, *Works of Knox*, VI, Part I, 78–79.

[51]Laing, *Works of John Knox,* IV, 358.

[52]See Collinson, *Elizabethan Puritan Movement,* p. 46.

[53]*Ibid.*, p. 118. See E. T. Bradley, *DNB*, VIII, 128–30.

[54]See Danner, "Christopher Goodman and the English Protestant Tradition of Civil Disobedience," *Sixteenth Century Journal* 8 (1977), 61–73. Cf. Althea Vadrienne Cherry, "The Life and Political Theories of Christopher Goodman," (M.A. Dissertation, University of Chicago, 1935), and Jane E. A. Dowson, "The Early Career of Christopher Goodman and His Place in the Development of English Protestant Thought," (Ph.D. Dissertation, University of Durham, 1978).

[55]British Museum Add. Ms. 32091, fos. 246–47; Bradley, *DNB,* VIII, 128–30.

[56]Collinson, *Elizabethan Puritan Movement,* pp. 210–11. Cf. Albert Peel, "A Sermon of Christopher Goodman's in 1583," *Journal of the Presbyterian Historical Society of England* 9 (1949), 80–93; Samuel J. Knox, "Christopher Goodman—A Forgotten Presbyterian," *Journal of the Presbyterian Historical Society* 28 (1950), 221–32.

[57]A. F. Pollard, *DNB*, LXI, 150–53; Anthony Wood, *Athenae Oxonienses,* P. Bliss, ed. (London: F.C.&J. Rivergton, 1813), I, 446–50.

[58]Garrett, pp. 327–30; see also Mary Anne Everett Green, ed., *Life and Death of Mr. William Whittingham, from a ms. in Anthony Wood's Collection,* Bodlein Library, Oxford (printed for the Camden Society, 1870), p. 3; and, J. Hay Colligan, *The Honourable William Whittingham of Chester* (London: Simpkin Marshall, 1934), *passim.*

[59]Pollard, *DNB,* LXI, 150–53. Cf. Danner, "Calvin and Puritanism: The Career of William Whittingham," *Calviniana. Ideas and Influence of Jean Calvin, Sixteenth Century Essays & Studies.*

[60]Garrett, p. 297; Mitchell, pp. 6, 12.

[61]Ridley's treatise bore the lengthy title, *Certen godly, learned, and/ comfortable conferences, betwene the two Reuerende Fathers, and holye martyrs of/Christ, D. Nicolas Rydley late Bysshoppe of London, and M. Hughe Latymer/ Sometyme Bysshoppe of Wor-/cester, during the time of theyr empryson-/ments. Whereunto is added./ A Treatise agayst the error of Transubstan-/tiation, made by the sayd Reuerende Father D./ Nicolas Rydley./* M.D.LVI (no colophon); Goodman's treatise, noted above, was *How Svperior Powers Oght to be Obeyd;* and, Beza's tract was *A Brief declaration of the chiefe poyntes of Christian Religion, set forth in a Table* (Geneva: Printed by Jo. Rivery, 1556).

[62]See Strype, *Parker*, III, 76–84; Collinson, *Godly People,* pp. 262–70.

[63]Cf. Wood's letter referred to above.

[64]Strype, *Grindal,* p. 145; Strype, *Parker*, I, 267–68.

[65]See Brook, I, 229–36.

[66]Strype, *Annals,* II, ii, 107–09.

[67]Strype, *Grindal,* pp. 252–53.

[68]Strype, *Annals,* II, ii, 167–74; cf. Green, pp. 47–48. There is no indication in the *Livre des Anglois* or any of the city council registers of Whittingham's ordination; this is the only source or reference to it of which I have knowledge. Garrett believes that as a result of the 1578 visitation, Whittingham was obliged to admit that he was no minister "according to the...ordinances of this realm," and that he had also been a "furtherer to the setting forthe of the wickcd book against the lawful regiment of women." See Garrett, pp. 327–30, who refers to *Camden Misc.* VI, Whittingham Appendix, II, p. 47.

[69]Wood, *Athenae Oxonienses,* I, 446–50.

[70]Mervyn James, *Family, Lineage and Civil Society: A Study of Society, Politics and Mentality in the Durham Region, 1500–1640* (Oxford: Clarendon Press, 1974), pp. 58–59.

[71]Garrett, p. 297; Mitchell, pp. 6, 11.

[72]Garrett, pp. 286–87.

[73]Mitchell, p. 6.

[74]Garrett, pp. 260–61.

CHAPTER 3

BISHOPS AND NOTABLE PURITANS WHO WERE MEMBERS OF THE GENEVA REFUGEE CHURCH

I. BISHOPS OF THE CHURCH OF ENGLAND WHO WERE MEMBERS OF THE GENEVA CHURCH

Four bishops were refugees in Geneva during the period 1555–60. Two of them, John Scory and Miles Coverdale, had been bishops in Edward's church. The other two were each made bishop during the Elizabethan Settlement. **James Pilkington** was the first of the future bishops to arrive in Geneva. The exact date of his arrival is not clear, but sometime between 10 November 1555 and 12 July 1556, Pilkington came to Geneva with another future Elizabethan prelate, John Scory.[1] Pilkington had been a fellow at St. John's, Cambridge, and was licensed to preach in 1547 along with Latimer, Cox, Horne, Sandys, Grindal and Knox. During Mary's reign, he was first seen on the Continent at Zurich. He enrolled as a student at Basel in the autumn of 1556, so his stay in Geneva was not a lengthy one. His name appeared as the first signatory of the letter sent by the Frankfurt church to Geneva in 1559, rejecting the proposal to hold a united front of anti-ceremonialism upon the exiles' return to the homeland.[2]

Once back in England, Pilkington became Bishop of Durham. He was a member of the committee commissioned to revise the Edwardian Prayerbooks, one of the first measures with which Cecil and company set about to constitute the Elizabethan Settlement. He had written during his university days at Cambridge a treatise on predestination, and although he may not have been in Geneva long enough to imbibe the full extent of the puritan sentiment there, his

demeanor as bishop within the Elizabethan Settlement was significant
and exceedingly helpful to puritans such as Whittingham.[3] In a letter
to the Earl of Leicester, 25 October 1564, he marveled that the vestment issue was so important to the Queen; Peter and Paul could agree
on salvation but differed on the question of eating meat, and Paul and
Barnabas could disagree about whether to take John Mark on their
second missionary journey. Why should vestments be made such an
important condition for preaching? Preachers were desperately
needed, and vestments gave no additional glory to God. Ordinary
people were confused to the point of not being able to distinguish a
Protestant preacher from a Catholic priest! Augustine had argued
many generations ago that no contentions should be made over such
things that might split believers. Pilkington also quoted Bucer's hu-
morous and rather famous line about never wearing a foursquare cap
on his round head, a line also quoted glibly by Anthony Gilby.[4]
Although Pilkington died in 1576, he insulated Whittingham from
many a trouble in Durham, and although he probably did not favor the
Genevans' radical ideas, either in substance or method, he nevertheless was a boon to the puritan cause.[5]

John Scory had come to Geneva at about the same time as
Pilkington, for both are mentioned in the *Livre des Anglois* in the
same entry, sometime between 10 November 1555 and 12 July 1556.
He stayed a short time. Prior to coming to Geneva, Scory had been at
Emden. Grindal had wanted him to become the minister for the
church at Frankfurt but he refused. He wrote *Epistle wrytten vnto all
the faithful that be in pryson in Englande* from Emden in 1555, in
which he exhorted Protestants at home with an apology for his own
defection during Mary's reign.[6] His activities as an exile are not easy
to follow, but it seems most likely that he returned to Emden to assume his duties as superintendent of the refugee church.

Scory was from Norfolk and during Henry VIII's reign he had been
a friar in the Dominican house at Cambridge. He signed the affidavit
to suppress the house in 1538. In 1541 he was one of six preachers
appointed to preach at Canterbury, and he served as chaplain to both
Cranmer and Ridley. As Bishop of Rochester, he was appointed by
Cranmer to the commission for the reform of ecclesiastical laws. The
same year he was appointed as Bishop of Rochester, 1551, Scory
preached a Lenten sermon in which he bemoaned the absence of
ecclesiastical discipline in England. Strype recounts an episode which
involved Scory: King Edward gave notice that Scory was preaching
when Joan Bocher was executed for heresy in May of 1550. On 23
May 1552, Scory was made Bishop of Chichester.[7]

When Mary ascended to the throne in 1553, Scory was deprived; he later recanted his Protestantism and was absolved under Bonner's seal on 14 July 1554. It was said of Scory that he placarded copies of Cranmer's declarations against the mass in the streets of London which made him at least partly responsible for Cranmer's imprisonment and eventual death. He was joined in the effort by John Ponet; both reformers fled to the Continent leaving the Archbishop to face the music alone.[8]

Upon Elizabeth's accession, Scory preached against the evils of Catholicism during Lent of 1559. He became one of the first bishops to be appointed by the Queen, having been given the see of Hereford on 15 July 1559.[9] He did not have an easy time as bishop, and complained bitterly in a letter to Parker that he was short of personnel— there were many chapels without clergy altogether, and some chapels were served only with readers. Scory signed the reformed articles of 1562–63 and the canons of 1571. He died a wealthy man on 26 June 1585 at Whitbourne.[10]

Scory's exile during Mary's reign gave him opportunity to translate two treatises of Augustine, *Two bokes of the noble doctor and B.S. Augustine theone entitled of the Predestination of saintes, thother of perserueraunce vnto thende.* In the preface, Scory explained that Pelagianism had been resurrected by Catholics and Anabaptists alike; St. Augustine indicated, in contrast, the true profession of free grace in Christ. Thus the accusation that the Augustinian doctrine of man preached during the reigns of Henry and Edward was a newfangled doctrine is unfounded. Augustine showed the proper stress of God's calling, and why some are called to salvation but not all. We frail human beings are weak and without divine aid we cannot find God or persevere in Him to the end. Salvation, then, was a matter of grace, and even our human response in faith is directed by God. We cannot be saved by our own doing and merit. These deep mysteries are known only to the eye of faith and there is nothing in human reason which can fathom them apart from faith. Augustine helps us to understand the doctrine of original sin, "the most just and secret judgment of God upon the children of wrath." The sacraments of the church, which remind us of these mysteries, are therefore necessary for salvation; that is why we baptize infants as an expression of our dependence upon the grace of God.

Scory found it comforting and enhancing that this was also St. Cyprian's position. Scory's conviction was that the true church of Christ persevered within the Church of England during the Henrican-Edwardian reforms, and that even though some ancient traditions of the church had been changed, the Church of England was on the surest of foundations when she built her thought and life on the scriptures. As long as no scriptural doctrine or practice of the primitive church was violated, the church of Scory's homeland would continue to perpetuate the legacy of apostolic Christianity. There was one thing, however, which gave Scory particular concern, and it deserved careful watching and conscientious implementation: ecclesiastical discipline. Otherwise, the English church did well to divorce itself from Catholicism which often practiced a form of Christianity unworthy of the name because of the lack of scriptural support. He mentioned specifically priests only drinking the cup and speaking a foreign language in church.[11]

Scory also translated *Certein workes of the blessed Cypriane the martyr, which was Bishop of Cartage* in 1556. The reason, he wrote in the preface, was that Cyprian's difficult time was so much like his own, doubtless a reflection of his own ambivalent feelings as a refugee bishop who regretted his past compromises of fidelity to the Protestant cause. Although his stay in Geneva was short, Scory is another example of a member of Elizabeth's clergy who was more than just a supporter of the Queen's religious policies. His puritanism, nurtured in exile and exposed for a short time to Genevan principles and practice, was not of a moderate variety which simply accepted as normative the wishes of the Queen for a via media between what she considered the best of both Catholicism and Protestantism.[12] His interest in predestination is one of the earliest examples of puritan interest in the subject. Perhaps his association with Pilkington and Gilby in Geneva, both of whom had written treatises on the subject, kindled his own interest. That this occurred in Geneva in the company and under the tutelage of Calvin is not without significance.

Thomas Bentham was in Geneva by 20 November 1557, and married Mawde Fawcon of Suffolk while there during the same year. Bentham had been a student of Magdalen College during the reigns of Henry and Edward, and was admitted perpetual fellow. He became Junior Dean of Arts in 1553 and received his D.D. in 1566 after his return from exile. He was an especially competent linguist, and his knowledge of Hebrew was well known.[13]

In the Fall of 1553, Stephen Gardiner had been commissioned to make a formal visitation to Oxford to cleanse the university of reformers. Bentham was among fourteen or fifteen who were affected by deprivation. He is said to have assisted Henry Bull who "openly in the choir shook the censer out of the hands of them that ministered." On 26 October, Bentham as junior dean was directed to correct absenteeism from masses. He said that he could not, and confessed his heartfelt sorrow for having complied with such idolatry during Henry's reign. Gardiner had him deprived of his fellowship.[14]

By April of 1554, Bentham was in Zurich. He signed the letter of reply to Frankfurt's invitation to join them. He was registered as a student for the year 1555–56 at Basel where he often preached. Bale included him in the list of those in *nostro collegio*. He left for Frankfurt where he sided with Horn against Ashley in their dispute, and eventually came to Geneva shortly thereafter.[15]

Bentham did not remain long in Geneva although his scholarship was probably a boon to those who were actively working on the complete edition of the Bible. He returned to London, from which he wrote to Lever on 17 July 1558. He indicated that he was preaching for the "exiled church" in London and wanted several questions answered by Peter Martyr if Lever could relay them to him. He informed Lever about what was happening in England, bemoaning particularly the matter of paying taxes to "evil rulers and wicked magistrates."[16] John Foxe gives an interesting account of Bentham's intercession for seven Protestants who were burned at Smithfield, and narrates another incident when Bentham refused to confirm a coroner's report because it required swearing upon "a papistical primer."[17]

After Elizabeth's accession, Bentham preached at St. Paul's on several occasions. At the age of forty-six, he was consecrated Bishop of Lichfield and Coventry on 24 March 1559. He signed to support the articles of religion in 1562–63, but his ecclesiastical office forced him to be somewhat indifferent to some of the more radical concerns of fellow puritans. He eventually, for example, came to view the vestments as adiaphora, although there was no little consternation about Elizabeth's orders for conformity in the diocese of Lichfield and Coventry. In 1565, a complaint had been registered and a visitation planned to investigate Bentham's diocese. He attempted to comply and played matters rather cozily, but the "dislike of habits" had become a considerable problem in Lichfield and Coventry.[18]

Bentham's pilgrimage is akin to many other puritans. Brought up in Henry's Anglo-Catholicism, he became remorseful of his past once he converted to Protestantism. Mary's accession would prove the need for exile, and Continental Protestantism would burn hotter to fashion a puritan fervor. When he returned to England after Elizabeth came to the throne in 1558, his education and erudition were needed for the Elizabethan Settlement, and without sacrificing the integrity of the faith, he thought, he could support the Protestant Queen out of necessity to participate in the national church's rejection of Catholicism. He came to this position as a member of Elizabeth's

prelates, but not without pain and ambivalence; still, he believed that
the Gospel would continue to be honored.[19]

But Bentham's brand of puritanism would not satisfy the more
radical members of the puritan movement, and from where they sat,
the Bishop had compromised the tenets of the faith and the purity of
the discipline he had been a part of on the Continent. In 1570,
William Axton, a contemporary of Cartwright at Trinity College,
Cambridge, was called before the Bishop of Lichfield and Coventry.
The cocky, confident Axton was adamantly opposed to the surplice
because it had been used by the papists and associated with idolatry,
and served no useful purpose. Bentham replied that these matters were
really indifferent, and since their sovereign stipulated their usage,
ministers ought to comply. Besides, the Elizabethan vestments were
not Roman and never had been used by papists. But a copy of a thing
is the same as the thing itself, Axton argued, whereupon, with tongue-
in-cheek, the Bishop said that he would willingly make the vestment
shorter or longer! Axton was convinced, however, that the surplice
was an offense to many, and for that reason Paul would enjoin that it
not be used. He voiced similar objections to the sign of the cross and
instrumental music in worship. Finally, the puritan informed Bentham
that he resented having to defend his position before an ecclesiastic
who was not ordained by consent of an eldership, or ordained over
one flock, or chosen by the congregation. Axton further denied that a
civil magistrate could preach or administer the sacraments, and when
the exchange reached the point of a dispute over the meaning of
Ezekiel 44, the Bishop brought out a Hebrew Bible and read the passage to Axton with sensitivity to the original text, at which juncture
the narrator of the story suggests that the dispute came to an end.
The narrator, puritan sympathizer that he was, laments that Bentham
"would have done well to have remembered these things when he became a lord bishop and a persecutor of his fellow protestants."[20]

The irony in this scene has to be viewed from within the ambivalence that Bentham felt, no doubt, for before he became an
Elizabethan bishop, the puritan Bentham had preached a sermon at St.
Peter's Church, Oxford on Matthew 4, the subject of which was the
temptation of Christ. It was published sometime later from London as
A Notable and comfortable exposition, vpon the fovrth of Mathew.
The theme of the sermon was that those in high places are more
prone to temptation. Among other points made, Bentham acknowledged that the Lenten fast was not grounded in scripture and cannot
be corroborated by reference to Christ's fasting, and that Lenten fasts
do not belong in the English church because they were not part of the
primitive church's practice. The sermon is replete with references to

the church fathers and Jewish history, and bears the marks of a gifted intellect. Little did Bentham realize that this sermon from his Oxford days at Magdalen would spell problems for an Elizabethan prelate accused of leaving his puritan past behind in exile. He died on 21 February 1579 and was buried in the chancel of the church in Staffordshire. His legacy included the work of translating Ezekiel and Daniel in the Bishops' Bible of 1568.[21]

The last of the bishops entered in the *Livre des Anglois* was **Miles Coverdale** who came to Geneva in the autumn of 1558. He is mentioned as a witness to the baptism of Knox's son on 29 November, and he became an elder of the church on 16 December 1558. He apparently stayed in Geneva until 14 August 1559, and probably gave some assistance in the work of the Geneva Bible, although he left before the project was finished. A letter to William Cole in Geneva written on 22 February 1560 from London contained Coverdale's encouragement to those who remained, and confirmation that he "thoroughly approve[d] of your plan of awaiting the opinion of Calvin in the rest of the chapters of Daniel also."[22]

Coverdale had become a Protestant by Lent of 1528. In 1529, he assisted Tyndale on the Continent with his translation of the Bible. He was probably with Tyndale in Wittenberg and Antwerp during the next year. It was in Antwerp in 1534–35 that he translated his own English Bible. He returned to England in 1535 and was commissioned to revise Matthew's Bible. He went to Paris in 1538, but was forced by the Inquisition to return to England. After the Six Articles were passed he again went across the channel. He married while abroad, and studied with Melanchthon at Wittenberg. He then went to Copenhagen as professor of divinity, then on to Strasburg where he stayed for about three years. In Strasburg, he formed a close relationship with Conrad Hubert, Bucer's secretary, who recommended him for a headmaster's position at Bergzabern. He was at Bergzabern as early as September 1543, although his travels in "lower Germany" gave him the opportunity to complete his D.D. in 1541 or 1542 from Tübingen. He may also have visited Denmark during this interlude since his wife, Elizabeth Macheson, had relatives there.[23]

After Henry VIII died, Coverdale wrote to Calvin on 26 March 1548 from Frankfurt that he was returning home to England by invitation. He was in England by 24 June 1548 when he preached at St. Martin's, Outwich. He became almoner to Queen Katherine and helped to translate Erasmus' *Paraphrases,* a project she had begun in 1545. When Katherine died, Coverdale preached her funeral sermon, and as the royal chaplain, he became associated with Thomas

Cranmer. Coverdale became one of the most notable preachers in England. He was in the company of Peter Martyr in 1551, and eventually was consecrated, in surplice and cope, as Bishop of Exeter on 30 August 1551. He was regular in attendance in his seat in the House of Lords, and was appointed among those who were to reform ecclesiastical laws and to investigate Anabaptism. Throughout Edward's reign he was an active reformer and preacher although he did very little writing during this time. He managed to translate a version of Otto Werdmuller's *Precious Pearl,* and a new edition of his 1535 Bible appeared in 1550.[24]

When Mary came to the throne, Coverdale was summoned to appear before the privy council on 22 August 1553. He was confined but probably not imprisoned, and he lost his bishopric the following September. His kinsmen in Copenhagen heard of his plight and the King of Denmark wrote letters to Queen Mary for his release. In time, Coverdale was allowed to go to Denmark; two servants were allowed to accompany him. He stayed but a few weeks before he left for Wesel, where he became chaplain, and then was invited to occupy his old post at Bergzabern. He arrived at Bergzabern via Frankfurt on 20 September 1555, and stayed two years. He then joined Lever and others from Wesel at Aarau before coming to Geneva during the autumn of 1558.[25]

At the accession of Elizabeth in 1558, Coverdale was seventy years of age. He officiated in black gown at the ordination of Parker, and was offered back his old bishopric which he refused. Instead, he preached for four years without preferment, although he surely was aided by his patroness, the Duchess of Suffolk. He became ill, but recovered to accept his D.D. from Cambridge by incorporation with Tübingen. In 1564, he acted in the place of the vice-chancellor in conferring the same degree on Grindal. He did not accept any other positions, probably because he was on opposite sides of the theological fence from the Elizabethans, until he was persuaded to take the living of St. Magnus by London Bridge on 6 March 1564. He resigned two years later. When the Advertisements came out the same month, Coverdale wrote to Parker's chaplain and asked for excuse from the summons because of ill health. His antipathy for vestments and other puritan taboos is clearly revealed in his correspondence to Reformers abroad. During the next two and a half years, Coverdale continued to preach; Richard Hooker gave a graphic account of his last sermon at St. Magnus when he had to be carried to the pulpit. He died in January of 1569.[26]

Coverdale's last book was *Certain most godly, fruitful, and comfortable letters of such true Saints and holy Martyrs of God,* written from London and published by John Day in 1564. Earlier in his career, he had translated works by Luther and Calvin, including the latter's *A Faithfvl and Most Godly treatyse concerning the most sacred sacrament of the blessed body and bloud of our Sauior Christ*, which the Genevan had written in 1540. In the preface to his translation, Coverdale acknowledged the contributions of Augustine against the doctrine of transubstantiation, and a number of themes in common with the annotations in the Geneva Bible of 1560 are apparent. In the second edition of the work, published by John Day from London about 1550, Coverdale's preface indicates that Calvin's view of the eucharistic presence had become his own: the sacrament, to become the body and blood of the Lord, had to be accompanied by faith. The second edition thus indicates that Coverdale's eucharistic theology was somewhat different from the theology of the Geneva Bible which is quite Zwinglian or sacramentarian; Coverdale's idea of the eucharist had moved toward a more Calvinist notion which would have been quite in keeping with Cranmer's thought. A similar position is reflected in an anonymous treatise written from Wittenberg in 1554, *The humble and vnfained confession of the beliefe of certain poore banished men* which Coverdale may have co-authored.[27]

The four bishops exiled in Geneva were there but a short time by comparison with the careers of Whittingham, Gilby and Goodman. None of the four bishops, with the exception of Coverdale who was quite older, could be labeled a radical puritan. But neither could they be called time-servers in total passive support of Elizabeth's via media. Pilkington, Scory and Bentham, being in responsible positions of ecclesiastical leadership in company with the crown, had to demonstrate careful but loyal behavior to England's national church of which Elizabeth was the "supreme governor." Both Pilkington and Scory were not happy prelates during the reign of Elizabeth, and both leaders would have been happier to see more of the puritan agenda, short of demanding a presbyterian form of church polity in the spirit of the *Admonitions,* implemented. It is not fair to keep the label "puritan" from these prelates, and although there may not have been a united front of Marian refugees who wanted to undermine the Elizabethan Settlement, these bishops were not unsympathetic to many of the concerns voiced by their erstwhile cohorts in exile. The one exception may have been Bentham. Interestingly, only Coverdale assumed any ecclesiastical and pastoral leadership role in the English church at Geneva. Already, then, a line of division was forming among those English Protestants in exile it is safe to name "puritan." But the label still sticks.[28]

II. NOTABLE DIVINES WHO WERE MEMBERS OF
THE GENEVA CHURCH

Geneva became a nurturing ground for many English Protestants, most of whom wanted to take the Reformation further in England toward a national church built on apostolic principles which they were convinced were exhibited on the Continent in the fairest fashion. That Geneva became for refugees who spent time there the paragon of Reformed doctrine, polity and discipline is clear from the way they lived and preached during Elizabeth's reign.

In the summer after the establishment of the refugee church, **Thomas Sampson** came to Geneva, arriving sometime before 12 July 1556. Sampson had studied at both Cambridge and Oxford, eventually taking degrees from the latter after he returned from exile. He was converted to the Protestant cause while a student at Cambridge. He and John Bradford received holy orders in 1549 from Bishop Ridley without having to assume the sacradotal habits. As the nephew of Hugh Latimer, he soon gained notoriety as a preacher. Along with Richard Chambers, he had collected money in London for the support of Protestant scholars at Cambridge and Oxford. Sampson became rector of Allhallows in 1551, and the year following he was preferred to the Deanery of Winchester.[29] His friend Bradford, along with Becon and Veron, was apprehended on 16 August 1554 and committed to the Tower. Sampson was supposed to have been apprehended also, but he was not to be found. He had already fled to Strasburg. It was from Strasburg in 1554 that he wrote to his former parishioners at Allhallows in London.[30] From correspondence, it can be discerned that he was in Strasburg in February of 1555 and the following April in Frankfurt. He spent some time in Lausanne and Zurich. In April 1558 he was in Frankfurt and back again at Strasburg the following July. By January of 1560 he had been a year back in England. It thus would appear that his tenure in Geneva was a short one, but his reputation as a Hebraist makes it highly plausible that he was consulted regarding the compilation of the Geneva Bible. His various travels as itinerant preacher among the English refugee churches would certainly facilitate his cooperation on the task. In a letter to Bullinger from Lausanne, 13 September 1556, he mentioned that he could always be contacted because Beza was in the habit of forwarding his letters to him.[31]

Although Sampson was adamantly opposed to any ceremony which smacked of Romanism, his earlier correspondence from the Continent would place him with Richard Cox as a moderate puritan.

In a letter to Calvin from Frankfurt, 5 April 1554, his name appears under Cox's with the affirmation that many ceremonies had been given up for the sake of harmony and good will. Private baptisms, confirmation of children, saints' days, and kneeling at the eucharist celebration were among things mentioned in the letter. The letter called these ceremonies indifferent matters, and the signatories were thus quite willing to omit them out of respect for those who were more scrupulous. The same message was communicated in Sampson's letter to Calvin the following year.[32] Clearly, Sampson sided with Cox in the troubles at Frankfurt and did not initially endorse the attitudes and policies of the Knox-Whittingham group which seceded from the Frankfurt church in flight to Geneva.

Sampson would change his mind, however, and his close association with Whittingham, Gilby, Knox and company at Geneva caused him to raise the question of what matters really were adiaphora and whether these, as defined by some, should be forced upon those who had difficulty in subscribing to them. Sampson was constantly writing Bullinger and Martyr and asking them to address these questions. He believed that Bucer had addressed himself to these questions in *De Regno Christi,* and now it was time for the contemporary leaders of the Rhineland Reformed churches to speak up. Moreover, his correspondence from England upon his return from exile shows that he continued to press these issues with the Rhinelanders when his more radical puritanism was the object of concern of both Elizabethans like Parker and also his fellow radicals such as Humphrey and Gilby.[33] The nuisance Sampson had become to Bullinger and Martyr is well attested in a letter from Bullinger to Beza on 15 March 1567:

> This however I freely confess to you, that I have always looked with suspicion upon the statements made by master Sampson. He is not amiss in other respects, but of an exceedingly restless disposition. While he resided amongst us at Zurich, and after he returned to England, he never ceased to be troublesome to master Peter Martyr of blessed memory. He often used to complain to me, that Sampson never wrote a letter without filling it with grievances: the man is never satisfied; he has always some doubt or other to busy himself with. As often as he began, when he was here, to lay his plans before me, I used to get rid of him in a friendly way, as well knowing him to be a man of a captious and unquiet disposition. England has many characters of this sort, who cannot be at rest, who can never be satisfied, and who have always something or other to complain about. I have certainly a natural dislike to men of this stamp.[34]

Back in England upon Elizabeth's accession, Sampson's career as a preacher continued to flourish. He wrote to Peter Martyr to tell him that Elizabeth had offered him a bishopric (Norwich), but he was fearful of having to compromise too much of what he had learned abroad. He wondered if he could conscientiously swear that the Queen was "the supreme head of the church under Christ," and the thought of having to wear ecclesiastical garb disturbed him. He did not like how bishops were appointed, without any congregational involvement or sanction, and governing in the Church of England without ecclesiastical discipline would be well nigh impossible. He informed Martyr that he would rather put his emphasis on preaching and not share in the government of the church until "he saw a thorough reformation, both in doctrine and discipline."[35]

Thus concentrating on preaching, he delivered the rehearsal sermons at St. Paul's Cross during the first three years of Elizabeth's reign. On 4 September 1560, he was installed Canon of Durham, and in March of the next year he appealed to attend the reading of St. Paul's epistles in anticipation of the B.D. at Oxford. In 1561, he was appointed Dean of Christ Church, Oxford. In November of 1561, he supplicated to preach in doctoral habit only. He sat in the convocation of 1562–63 and voted in favor of the puritan agenda in support of the articles to reform religion and abolish certain rites and ceremonies. He also signed the petition in the lower house for ecclesiastical discipline. He declined to wear vestments and ecclesiastical garb, and on 3 March 1564, Sampson, Humphrey and four other puritan preachers were cited to appear before the ecclesiastical commission at Lambeth. Here Parker, who along with Sandys, Grindal and Bradford had been extensively consulted by Bucer in the composition of *De Regno Christi* as fellows of Pembroke Hall, advised the preachers to acquiesce to the wearing of vestments because such was the advise of not only Bucer, but Peter Martyr, Bullinger and Gualter as well. But the preachers, with Sampson as spokesman, would not acquiesce, whereupon Cecil was called in and the ministers were required to stay until a resolution was forthcoming.

Their stay prolonged for several weeks. They then drafted a letter to Parker, with copies to other bishops, in which they raised the question: if such ecclesiastical attire is adiaphora, why press the matter to the point of inconvenience? Did the prelates not have better things to do with their time and energy on behalf of their flocks? They were not condemning those who thought that the wearing of vestments was an indifferent matter, so why were they being vexed because of their scrupulosity against them? The ministers believed that the practice of the primitive church was on their side and that Reformed churches abroad would corroborate their position. Sampson and the ministers also sent a letter to the Earl of Leicester in which they expressed the need to be back at their respective colleges. They would conform, they said, because it was not their intention to be trouble-makers or separatists, but they needed to make their decision in the homely environment of "God and learning."[36]

By the 29th day of March, they were informed that they could not go home and that unless they complied they would be deprived of their offices. They were required to wear the cap, to wear no hats with their long, academic gowns, to wear a surplice with non-regent's hoods in the choirs of their colleges, and to kneel at communion where wafer bread was to be used. The ministers said that their consciences would not allow them to comply. Parker relayed the proceedings to Cecil who would, in turn, inform the Queen; the Queen would then send word concerning the deprivation of their offices.[37]

Nothing seems to have happened immediately. The Earl of Leicester had perhaps interceded for them, or others in high places had put in a good word on their behalf. Easter was approaching and they were even asked to preach at Paul's Cross! In December of 1564, the same year, an extensive exchange took place between Parker and Sampson and Humphrey. Nine questions were put forward by the Archbishop and each was answered by the preachers with copious documentation from the scriptures and church fathers. Parker asked whether the surplice was inherently evil or a matter of adiaphora. Sampson's answer was that it would be a matter which needed weighing in context; it would not be indifferent if there were any idolatrous association. What about a bishop enacting the use of such an ecclesiastical vestment as a matter of official requisition? Should not ministers obey the order of one who was admittedly a fellow Protestant in such an exigency? The answer from the preachers was to be expected: no minister of the Gospel should obey an order which he conscientiously believed to be a "patch of popery" and which was "clearly used for pomp and effect." Parker inquired about the cope, was it a matter indifferent? It, too, was papistical and served only to "dress up the sacrament" by defacing it; why would God disallow gold from the temple "for reverence and decency" in the apostolic church yet condone the same kind of superstition left as a vestige in the English church from Catholicism?

Parker could see that he was getting nowhere, so he probed a vulnerable area for puritans: what about the magistrate of the realm—could she proclaim a day of fasting from meat? Yes, the preachers admitted, as long as no "superstition" was associated with such an order. Parker wanted to learn if the ministers thought there should be any distinction between clergy and laity and whether such a distinction should be exemplified in apparel. Sampson and Humphrey answered that the primitive church made no such distinctions. Would they condemn a church which made such a distinction and exemplified such with special clerical apparel, then? No, they said, only God can judge. And on the argument went.[38]

The anti-vestiarian stance of scrupulous puritans like Sampson and Humphrey was clearly that if such matters were adiaphora, and recognized as such by the Queen's men, then they cannot by the intrinsic nature of what is indifferent and only expedient be made the crux of a perforced conformity. When they were forced upon them, ministers who were kindred spirits with Sampson and Humphrey would not conform. In effect, to them these matters were not indifferent, and that was a crucial distinction in puritan hermeneutics. If those in power maintained that wearing of vestments was indeed adiaphora, then it should be exclusively optional as to whether they were worn or not, depending upon the conscience or degree of scrupulosity of the clergy involved. Interestingly, the position of the puritan mentors on the Continent, including Bullinger, Martyr, Gualter, and even Calvin and Beza, was that the vestments were not edificatory at all, and some of the reformers, particularly Beza and Gualter, were quite offended by them. But precisely because vestments were adiaphora, it was not the kind of controversy worth losing one's liberty to preach the Gospel; rather like winning the battle but losing the war.

Neither Parker nor Grindal could persuade the preachers to conform, Grindal urging them "with tears in his eyes." Sampson would be made a test-case because his position at Christ Church was considered crucial and exemplary by Elizabeth and her cohorts. He was thus deprived and Humphrey, after a confinement in London, was allowed to return home. Some ten years later, to the chagrin of his fellow radical puritans, Humphrey complied and wore the habits. Sampson was never imprisoned, but he was nevertheless deprived of the liberty to preach and administer the sacraments. He implored Parker to help him retrieve the liberty to preach, and the Archbishop glibly promised to do what he could. The Earl of Huntington interceded for Sampson at this juncture, June of 1565, and Parker informed him that he would be free to pursue his preaching again. Such was the good fortune of what Strype calls the "peaceable non-conformists" in contrast with those who became absolute separatists from the national church; it was the latter who radicalized even further the legacy of the Geneva exiles by setting up their separatist churches on the basis of the *Forme of Prayers and Administration of the Sacraments* which the English refugees had formulated in 1556 at Geneva.[39]

In 1567, Sampson became Master of Wigston's Hospital at Leicester. Later he was given mastership of Whittington College,

London, where he lectured each term and was supported by a stipend from cloth workers. In 1572 or 1573, he was stricken with palsy which paralyzed one side of his body and retired to Wigston's Hospital. Before his death in 1589, he continued to support the puritan cause through writing and correspondence, although he confided to Gilby in 1584 that Gilby's estimation of his ability and interest in setting down a "platform of reformation" was misplaced; his main concern was that an assembly of concerned divines gather and discuss the matter in the presence of government representatives. In such an assembly, Sampson said that he could "find in mine heart to be a doorkeeper, though it were only to keep out dogs."[40] Much of his correspondence was with the treasurer, Lord Burghley (before 1571, William Cecil), frequently if not constantly urging him to promote a reformation ala Bucer's recommendations in *De Regno Christi*. In 1583, he sent to Burghley via his son certain petitions relating to the reformation of ecclesiastical matters, particularly the matter of ecclesiastical discipline. A year later, he reissued them to present to the Queen and Parliament in a tract entitled, *A supplication made in the name of certain true subjects.*[41]

Grindal did not consider Sampson (and Humphrey) to be the radical kind of puritan mirrored in the *Admonition*.[42] But there was little difference between Gilby and Sampson. That Sampson spent only a short time in Geneva and never served the church in any pastoral or ministerial capacity is not without significance. Much of his theology bears a resemblance to the Whittingham-Knox tradition, exemplified by Gilby, but there are important nuances which need to be recognized.[43] It is strange, indeed, how some events take a turn. That Sampson was initially at odds with the Whittingham-Knox party at Frankfurt, or that he was able to absorb more of the Rhineland theology, especially in his exchanges with Bullinger, Peter Martyr and Gualter, during his experience in exile—these are matters difficult to interpret in the broader context of his career as a puritan divine.

Back home in England during the reign of Elizabeth, he clearly was on Elizabeth's (or at least Cecil's) list of qualified leaders who could assist in the Elizabethan Settlement, and he never tired of extending himself to those in authority, particularly Cecil, with mandates for carrying further the Protestant Reformation. Was he too close to the government for the *Admonition* crowd? Did he feel it necessary to disassociate himself from the radical political ideas of Knox and Goodman? It is nevertheless without doubt that Geneva had changed his perspective irrevocably, and he had the highest regard for Calvin of any of the Geneva exiles.[44]

William Kethe was a Scotsman whose name appears in the *Livre des Anglois* along with his wife in the entry of 5 November 1556. The Registre des Habitants of Geneva described Kethe as "a native from Exeter," adding to the confusion of his Scottish identity. He did not originally come to Geneva with the Knox-Whittingham party,[45] although he did sign the farewell letter of the disaffected followers of Whittingham when they took leave of Frankfurt. Kethe apparently traveled to Basel where he may have been in John Foxe's company, but he eventually settled with the Geneva refugees, and became a resident of the city on 7 January 1557. Late in the summer of 1557, he traveled with John Bodley in search for a new home for the refugee congregation at Wesel which was eventually established at Aarau.

Kethe was the poet of the English church. One of the first pieces written by him was a small tract entitled *Unto the ryghte honorable the nobilitie and ientlemen of Englande*, later called Kethe's "Seeing Glass." It provided a mirror for the rich and powerful to look into to see how the mighty can fall when they heed not the preaching of the gospel. Kethe reflected on Alsop's Fable of the Fox and the Goat and how it reflected the situation in Marian England. The exiles' homeland, like the goat in the pit, had her clothes stained with the filth of the fox in his attempt to lift her out. The fox would not be faithful to his promise to rescue the goat, for the very ones England should esteem were being murdered. The fox was using her as his hangman! Changing his metaphor, Kethe likened England to a "widow that was sometimes a flower of all nations" but now has been "brought under tribute, which sometime ruled all lands." Kethe commended to those suffering under papal rule a little book, "The Spiritual and Precious Pearl, set forth by the Duke of Sommerset," as an appropriate resource of comfort during a time when so many were wavering and insecure about the direction their nation was going.[46]

In 1557 he wrote a poem which likely reflected Mary Tudor's political problems. According to John Strype, in March of 1556, Philip had come to England and was given the grand tour by Mary's nobles. Philip advised Mary to break off relations with France and to support him with soldiers to "go over and annoy that dominion."[47] In the process, Calais was lost to the French. Philip needed London support to recapture Calais, and Strype believed that these events were hinted in Goodman's *How Svperior Powers Oght to be Obeyd*. Kethe's poem, however, made the reference explicit. Although there is no evidence to support Strype's claim, Kethe's poem was a powerful reflection of Mary's political problems with France and Spain; Kethe's caricature of Mary's plight is given a strong dose of divine retribution for the Queen's sins.[48]

Kethe was in Strasburg on 3 January 1559, Aarau on 16 January of the same year but he returned to Geneva to assist in the completion of the Geneva Bible in 1560. He went to England in 1561, where he was instituted to the rectory of Okeford, Dorset. He accompanied the Earl of Warwick on his expedition to Newhaven in 1563 as a minister. Here he preached to the English army. In 1569, he went to the "north parts" again as a preacher to military troops engaged in "subduing the popish rebels." In 1571, Kethe published *A Sermon made at Blanford Forum* which was printed and dedicated to the Earl of Warwick. In the preface he reminisces about his experiences with the earl in Newhaven as preacher to military troops. He mentioned that while in these "north parts" he practiced "a certain kind of discipline even upon those, that by birth and parentage, were far above me."

The sermon was a neat, three-pointed overview of Kethe's assessment of the Elizabethan Settlement, and how he as a former Marian exile in Geneva was able to function within it. He believed it was the duty of magistrates to uphold religion, to protect innocent ministers of the gospel, and to punish evildoers. The sabbath should be sacrosanct, never desecrated by ordinary work or profanation with "bullbeatings, bear-beatings, bowlings, dicing, carding, dancing, drunkenness and whoredom." Kethe expressed that many good things had been accomplished during Elizabeth's reign, but he was puzzled why so many Protestant ministers were being deprived or arrested for exposing papistical doctrine. And most of the time the ministers were charged with accusations that go four or five years back in time.[49]

Kethe denied that he ever advocated cruelty to magistrates. God has always abhorred tyranny. "It is a miserable common weal where it is lawful for a man to do nothing, but more miserable...where every man may do what he list."[50] Still, he was convinced that reformers were never given the tolerance that Catholics in his neck of the woods were given. There still were remnants of popery to uproot. Catholic ministers still failed to read the scriptures, in spite of what the Queen had dictated, and parishioners scarcely knew a word of the Bible in English. Many people continued to hide their "monuments of idolatry" in their houses.

It thus appears that Kethe continued with the puritan agenda he learned first-hand in Geneva. Time and the familiarity of home had mellowed him somewhat, for he clearly vacillated on whether he still would support the radical political theology of Knox and Goodman, the controversial books of whom he had given sanction with his own literary genius. Yet he seems to be fairly far removed from the loop of the more radical puritans who were pushing for the extremes indicated in the *Admonition* of 1572. Kethe probably died in 1608.[51]

William Kethe is mainly remembered for his metrical psalms, his version of the one-hundredth Psalm ("All People that on Earth do Dwell") still sung from many Protestant hymnals today. He wrote twenty-five metrical psalms in all, first printed in the English Psalter at Geneva in 1561. They were subsequently transferred to the Scottish Psalter of 1564; only ten or so were adopted in the English Psalter of 1562. His ninety-fourth Psalm was appended to Knox's *Appellation*. The famous one-hundredth Psalm appeared in the appendix to the 1562 Psalter but was admitted into the text of the 1585 edition.[52]

In addition, the gifted exile wrote some popular ballads, such as "A Ballet, declaring the fal of the whore of Babylone, intytuled Tye thy Mare, Tomboye...." He produced a poem highlighting Goodman's controversial *How Svperior Powers Oght to be Obeyd*, and a poem written in the form of a ballad which depicts the late Henrican period, "Of misrules contending/with gods worde by name, and then/of ones Judgment/ that heard of the same." Much of the work of the English Psalter was the work of Kethe and Whittingham, the latter having played a more dominant and influential role. Even so, Kethe's contribution to the puritan cause and perpetuation of the Geneva legacy should be given more attention than it has to date.[53]

Percival Wiburn (Wiburne) is named in the city registers of Geneva as a student. He was in Geneva by 7 May 1557. He formerly had been at St. John's Cambridge, having been admitted on 11 November 1546 and graduated B.A. in 1551. In 1552, he was a fellow at St. John's. He seems not to have remained long in Geneva, for he returned to England at Elizabeth's accession. He went back to St. John's, proceeded with the M.A. in 1558, and became in the same year junior dean and philosophy lecturer. After several livings he was installed canon of Westminster in November 1561.[54]

Wiburn took part in the Convocation of 1562–63 and subscribed to the revision of the articles. He was eventually sequestered for nonconformity, and in 1566, he was the emissary for other puritans to the Continent where he visited with Beza and Bullinger. In June of 1571, he was again cited for nonconformity before Archbishop Parker, and was examined in 1573 for possible involvement in the authorship of the *Second Admonition* which he denied. He was nevertheless forbidden to preach. Later, his privilege was restored, and in the 1580s he was actively involved in disputations with Catholics.[55]

Wiburn was an Erastian when it came to judging Catholic loyalty to the crown, and his support of Elizabeth and her office as governor of the church is quite evident; not all puritans were tyrannicidal although they were all vehemently anti-Catholic. In fact, Wiburn was especially appreciative of Calvin's political ideas and commended the last chapter of the fourth book of the *Institutes* where the "excellent dignity of civil princes and Magistrates" was championed along with the necessity of civil obedience. Doubtless sensitive to his vulnerability by association with erstwhile Geneva exiles who had advocated quite an opposite political theology, Wiburn contended that Calvin had said the last word. John Jewell's *Apology* could be read with the same profit.[56]

Wiburn, however, again found himself in trouble with the Elizabethans. He was suspended by Whitgift in 1583 for nonconformity and continued under suspension for the next five years. He eventually was allowed to preach, even with a broken leg, before he died in 1606. Was he a radical puritan? It has been suggested that he was,[57] but his radical stance was not as left-wing as many of his contemporaries or fellow Geneva refugees. Even so, his career though checkered in the last two decades was one which hardly acquiesced to the Queen's desires for an Anglican clergy and conformity to Romish vestments. Such things were too close to Rome and too far from Jerusalem and Antioch.[58]

John Pullein was in Geneva with his wife and daughter by 5 June 1557. He was elected deacon of the English church while there. A native of Yorkshire, he had studied at New College, Oxford where he was granted both the B.A. and M.A. degrees. He was ordained a deacon in November 1550, and a priest the following year; he was made rector of St. Peter's, Cornhill in 1552. He was deprived in April 1555. There has been speculation that he had left for Geneva in 1554, but was secretly back in England living under a pseudonym and acting as chaplain to the Duchess of Suffolk and holding services at Colchester and Cornhill. When Bonner discovered him, he escaped to Geneva. This speculative but intriguing story is based on Barlett Green's confession which John Foxe included in his *Acts and Monuments*: Green had reported that Pullein was with Goodman and later Michael Reniger "at his own house" celebrating "two eastertides."[59]

Before he arrived in Geneva, Pullein had been in Basel where he was arrested for not having a passport. He was well-known as a linguist and poet, and probably could have aided in the composition of the Geneva Bible. He was also known to have turned into metre Psalms 148 and 149.[60] Pullein did not remain long in Geneva, however, for he went back to England shortly after Elizabeth's accession.

He immediately got into trouble with the Elizabethans and was apprehended on 17 April 1559.

Grindal had favored him for the archdeanery of Colchester, and later that same year, 1559, he became rector of Copford in Essex. He eventually resigned and was installed as prebendary at St. Paul's Cathedral. He signed the articles against Romish ceremonies as well as the petition for ecclesiastical discipline in 1562–63.[61] Pullein was known by John Bale as a theologian and literary scholar. Bale reported that Pullein had written a theological treatise against Arianism and was the author of several historical renditions of apocryphal literature.[62]

Another notable puritan preacher spent a short stay in Geneva. **Lawrence Humphrey** is mentioned in the *Livre des Anglois* as being a member of the English church on 8 April 1558. He did not remain long and played little if any role in the developments there. As a Marian exile, he had spent time in both Zurich and Basel before he came to Geneva. He was enrolled at the University of Basel in 1555, and after he left Geneva, he returned to Basel from which he left on 23 June 1559 to return to England. He was appointed Regius Professor of Divinity at Oxford and eventually assumed the presidency of Magdalen College. He was later Dean of Gloucester in 1571–80, and Dean of Winchester in 1580. He died in 1589 and was buried in Magdalen College chapel.[63]

It will be recalled that Humphrey and Sampson were embroiled in the vestment controversy, having been cited to appear before Parker at Lambeth in March of 1564. Both divines refused to conform to the wearing of ecclesiastical vestments for which they were held in confinement. Humphrey was imprisoned in 1565. He would eventually write to Cecil to intercede on his behalf to the Queen. In time, Elizabeth came to Oxford, where Humphrey, dressed in scarlet habits, got to kiss her majesty's hand. Elizabeth responded with gentle but cutting words: "Methinks this gown and habit becomes you very well, and I marvel that you are so straight-laced on this point—but I come not to chide."[64]

Royal charm must have had its effect, for when he became Dean of Gloucester Humphrey consented to wear the habits. In 1575, he was instrumental in having several puritans expelled from the college for nonconformity. To the chagrin of his erstwhile Geneva exiles, the remainder of his career was a repetition of his acquiescence to the Elizabethan Settlement.

Humphrey was a gifted writer and felt at home in several languages. His humanist scholarship produced the *Life of Jewell*, which brought him wide acclaim. But two tracts written from Basel in 1559, just after Knox's *First Blast* and Goodman's *How Svperior Powers Oght to be Obeyd* had been published at Geneva, deserve special attention. In the most important of the two tracts, *De religionis conservatione et reformatione vera*, Humphrey commended the model of the church he had seen first-hand in exile. He called for a separation of state and church and gave qualified acceptance of female sovereignty. Like many of his Reformed mentors, he was quite explicit concerning the role of parliament and lesser magistrates in the event of an ungodly ruler: no private or individual resistance should be condoned, for the responsibility resides with lesser magistrates to bring about a more just order. Humphrey even went so far as to argue that both Knox and Goodman, their language understandably harsh, would agree with his point-of-view, and that rather than refuting their arguments it was best to try to understand and explain them.[65]

The other Basel treatise, *Optimates,* was a discourse on the nature and duties of the nobility, called by Knappen "a gesture in the direction of the rising class of Protestant landlords, soliciting their cooperation in the great work of reformation which lay ahead."[66] Not much of Humphrey's later theology, church polity or political philosophy would endear him to those with whom he shared a few brief months in Genevan exile. He had become a moderate puritan whose next easy step was as an Anglican.[67]

III. OTHER NOTABLE PURITANS WHO WERE MEMBERS OF THE GENEVA CHURCH

In addition to prelates and notable preachers, there were other outstanding puritan personalities who were members of the refugee church. Many of them played significant roles in the puritan cause, and not a few of them wanted to take the reformation further than the Elizabethan Settlement. Each of the following is mentioned in the *Livre des Anglois*; we should look at them according to how long they remained in Geneva as members of the English church. Again, it will be important to observe their careers not only while they were members of the Geneva church but also to study their later activities when their Geneva experience was bearing fruit in the vineyard of the Elizabethan Settlement.

Robert Beaumont, the Cambridge graduate from Leicestershire, had accompanied Pilkington to Geneva, arriving before the summer

of 1556. He was made a resident on 14 October 1557. Before coming
to Geneva, he had first gone to Zurich, for he signed that church's letter in answer to the Frankfurt congregation's invitation to join
them.[68] Upon his return to England in 1560, Beaumont was named
Lady Margaret Professor of Divinity at Trinity College, Cambridge,
where he proceeded with his B.D. He later became master of Trinity
College and received his D.D. in 1564. Elizabeth was present at his
doctoral disputation. Before his death he had been named a second
time vice-chancellor of the university.[69]

Beaumont had subscribed to the articles of 1562–63 and supported
the six articles on discipline. He wrote letters as university administra-
tor to Parker and Cecil imploring them to encourage the Queen to
drop the requisition of the surplice. When they responded with no little displeasure, even becoming irate, Beaumont backed down saying he
was only representing the opinion of some, not necessarily his own.
He thenceforth wrote a letter of submission to Cecil.[70]

Beaumont had corresponded with Anthony Gilby during the
decade of the 1560s, and the words between two former Geneva exiles
were not always pleasant. Gilby chided and rebuked Beaumont for not
maintaining the steadfastness that Gilby thought necessary of a reformer of popish ceremonies, accusing him of returning to the "toys
of popery," and setting up "bristles against God's faithful servants."
Neither the ancients at Cambridge nor Calvin in Geneva would ap-
plaud his behavior. Apparently Gilby had also accused Beaumont of
enjoying too much material splendor as a result of caving in to the
pressures of the Elizabethans. Beaumont's answer was more than interesting. He said that he did not see anything particularly wrong in
the Second Edwardian Prayerbook, certainly nothing he would call
"superstitious" (a loaded term for many puritans), and that he had
allowed the surplice to be worn "all opinion of holiness, necessity and
worship set apart." He acknowledged to Gilby that he himself wore
only the square cap and surplice although he had made more than one
request to be free even from these. The rationale for his acquiescence
was not, however, the appeal to be subject to those in authority, but
rather the practical exigency of preaching.

He had thus recently concluded that those who wore such habits
without pang of conscience should not be discriminated. He was
amused by Gilby's accusation of materialism. After all, he was still
riding the same old horse (albeit his tail had been cut off!) and his diet
was as it had always been, beef, bacon and cold milk. In fact, retorted
Beaumont, his expenses were just about what they were when he was a
student, never more than 4d per week. He confessed that matters were
not as they ought to be at Trinity, but he was working to try and im-

prove them. He had already gotten rid of capes, purged windows of Catholic icons, eliminated crucifixes, vestments, altarclothes and candlesticks. The only reason he continued to wear the surplice himself was in order to preach; the surplice was not worth being denied to preach the gospel. Even Augustine should help us to learn as much.[71]

Beaumont's will avowed his salvation by grace through faith, and stipulated that he was not to buried with the "jangling of bells and other popish ceremonies."[72] Here was a puritan very sensitive to the Geneva legacy, but whose position of influence and authority necessitated taking a few steps toward moderation. Such steps would gain him the chafing from those less pragmatic and more idealistic, but Beaumont still represents the heart of the puritan ethos—a return to the gospel, the emphasis on preaching and the consequent edification of the godly, and the purification of the church of what Rome had added to the apostolic pattern.

William Fuller arrived in Geneva during July of 1556. His wife probably died while he was there. He became a resident of the city in January 1557, and was appointed both an elder and deacon in the English church. He signed the letter of 15 December 1558 which had been written by the Geneva church to their sister churches in exile encouraging one and all to keep the faith, get rid of the prayerbook, and maintain steadfastness in pursuing Reformed theology and piety upon their return to England.[73] Fuller was true to the words of the epistle, for Thomas Wood wrote to Whittingham in February of 1573 that Fuller had been imprisoned for denying subscription to the prayerbook.[74]

Before he went into exile, Fuller seems to have been a member of Elizabeth's household at Hatfield and to have assisted the Queen in all her "heavy journeys" even riding with Elizabeth's sister on her way to the Tower. Fuller went into exile, he said, until he could be assured by the folks at Hatfield that it was safe to return to England. He became chagrined to learn that the Queen had "altered her mind and manners" to such an extent that Fuller felt the necessity to stay longer in Geneva, his "joy turned into mourning." So despondent, he resolved to remain in Geneva the rest of his life, until Calvin convinced him to return home.[75]

Because of his personal knowledge of and affection for the Queen, Fuller was convinced that he could change her mind. He prepared for her a French edition of the Bible (the 1560 Geneva Bible was not yet completed), the *Forme and Prayers*, which was the church order of the Geneva church, and a small New Testament, likely Whittingham's 1557 edition. Returning to London on 27 February 1559, Fuller had hoped for a personal audience with her majesty, and attempted to have a former associate, Thomas Parry, the treasurer of the Queen's household, to intercede on his behalf. Parry informed Fuller that the Queen was extremely irritated with the controversial book by Christopher Goodman advocating civil disobedience and denigrating female sovereigns. Parry suggested that Goodman had crept back into England, at least if rumor could be believed, and that Fuller might disclose his whereabouts. That would ingratiate him to Elizabeth, which in turn would put Fuller in good stead for a visit. Meanwhile, the authorities were looking for Goodman. But Fuller did not know where Goodman was, nor was he ever sympathetic to Goodman's (and Knox's) political theology. Those closest to Goodman and knew of his hiding would never vouchsafe information to Fuller.

Elizabeth was nevertheless convinced that she could get to Goodman through Fuller, and she asked Parry to press Fuller for information. Thomas Mildmay, the sheriff of Essex, brought John Pullein to Parry; Pullein had been known to have endorsed publicly Goodman's radical ideas. During the meeting of these principals, Pullein accused Fuller of jeopardizing the lives of Goodman, Knox and even himself. Fuller, hurt, responded that he had nothing but sincere love for his fellow exiles, and that he never intended to jeopardize them in any way. Fuller was especially fond of Knox, he said, for the Scot had taught him "many heavenly lessons and spiritual good things." It is certainly plausible that the accusation attributed to Pullein against Fuller had been a concoction of the sheriff in order to unnerve Fuller.[76]

The result of these events did in fact unnerve Fuller, but not in a way that the Queen had hoped. He decided against having an audience with her. He was miffed that the books he sent as a gift had neither been received nor acknowledged, and the confession of his faults to her majesty was thus never understood or appreciated. He knew that Elizabeth had little respect for Geneva, or for Calvin; the latter was as responsible as anyone for creating "precisians" of the English refugees who spent time there. As Fuller gave further reflection, his own Geneva experience had meant too much to see it compromised, even by the Queen whom he had known personally. Therefore he prepared a long list of accomplishments attributable to Geneva and the English church and contrasted it with Elizabeth's via media. Because she favored popish innovations such as vestments, altars, crosses, candlesticks, tapers and images, God would bring punishment upon the realm. Why the Queen should judge the whole Geneva church, and all that was accomplished there, by the "two faults" of two ministers who wrote two books was more than he could comprehend. If Elizabeth would just be still and reflect—neither Calvin, nor the English refugee church, nor the whole city were in sympathy with the sentiments expressed in those books![77]

Fuller would remain aloof, admitting to periods of depression, from Elizabeth until January 1579. Because he was concerned about who might be appointed as members of the privy council, he requested to see the Queen. His request was honored and he discussed with Elizabeth some of his concerns. The conversation seemed amicable, and the Queen advised him to put his concerns in writing. He did, adding a second set of concerns about Parliament's dubious financial acts which resulted in financial deprivation for the Queen.[78]

Fuller saw Elizabeth again, this time at her request. The meeting was on 19 February 1579, and the two discussed what Fuller had put in writing. He expressed special concern about "antichristians" who "would be made councilmen." He pressed Elizabeth's patience still further, delivering as he was to term it, "a brief admonition." This amounted to a heavy dosage of Deuteronomic retributive justice doused with apocalyptic fervor. In this "last and worst age of the world," Elizabeth had the opportunity to throw out antichrist, get rid of Romism, and set a course of reformation. God had so preserved her for this hopeful hour

> that were unworthy by reason of your yielding to that idolatry, and set you upon this mighty Imperial seat, not only to set out his glory, manifest his revealed will, increase and maintain his church and kingdom, but also to deface and put down that most monstrous and deceitful antichrist.[79]

Fuller went on to suggest that the Queen had not done enough to get rid of Romanism within the Church of England, her efforts being "neither hot nor cold." Instead of a coronation by "God's holy ministers" she had allowed antichristian bishops to perform the rite. She continued to attend mass; moreover, she perpetuated the idolatrous practice of the eucharist, and endorsed the presence of Roman images and icons. The puritan became even more insensitive to his Queen: she was known to have sworn in her anger and treated the Christian sabbath as no different than any other day. Fuller's insensitivity got political: some of the Queen's subjects "have been killed in Spain for the Word of God," yet she "hath never in the zeal of God executed here any of their idolaters." What was to become of a nation under God's favor which had this kind of leadership? Fuller feared the worst. Elizabeth must confess her faults, repent and turn to God in order that his wrath might not rain down plagues upon her majesty's realm.[80]

It is no surprise that Fuller could not get a visit with Elizabeth after he delivered his "brief admonition." Nor could he count on Parry's assistance any longer. He later decided to write to Elizabeth a letter which included a short prayer that her majesty might pray to receive forgiveness. On 13 July 1585 he requested Lady Leighton to intercede, only to be put off by Elizabeth—she had heard enough—who sent a representative. Fuller said that he had to see and talk to the Queen herself because "there are matters which cannot be spoken of before 'a secondary person'." If matters had deteriorated this much, he could perforce talk to several members of the privy council.[81]

Fuller recounted these events in 1586. They reveal intriguing perceptions of Elizabeth from a Geneva refugee who had been profoundly influenced by his experiences, experiences which were too important for him to compromise or to have a personal acquaintance ignore, even if she were the queen of England and supreme governor of England's national church. Why could she not see the importance of taking the reformation farther?

Another puritan figure who was a member of the Geneva refugee church was **John Bodley**. Bodley was received with his wife, three sons and a daughter, a brother, and three servants by the English church on 8 May 1557. Another son was born while he was in Geneva.[82] The following June he was made a resident of Geneva and on 31 May 1558 Bodley was received as a burgher. He was of the family of Bodleigh of Dunscombe-by-Crediton, and his wife was an heiress to both fame and fortune. Thomas, their son, was the founder of the Bodlein Library. In 1549, John Bodley had helped to finance the suppression of the rebellion in Devon against the introduction of the First Edwardian Prayerbook.[83]

Bodley had gone abroad because of his Protestant leanings. His son, in his autobiography, reported of his father being treated cruelly for his religious views.[84] He was first seen on the Continent in Wesel, then Frankfurt, before arriving in Geneva. He went with Kethe to assist the exiles of Wesel to find a new home in Aarau. He, along with William Williams, helped to set up a printing office at Geneva, and he gave to Rowland Hall the direction of printing the Geneva Bible of 1560. On 16 December 1557 he was elected an elder of the English church.[85] Twenty years later, Bodley would serve as an elder in the French "Strangers' Church," one of several London churches in which he was active. He was an overseer of the will of Richard Culverwell who had given money in support of the French immigrants.[86]

While in Geneva, Bodley's son Thomas studied Hebrew, Greek and theology, and attended lectures by Chevalerius, Berealdus, Calvin and Beza. Young Thomas was living in the house of a Genevan physician, Philibertus Saracenus.[87] The Bodleys returned to London, leaving Geneva on 5 September 1559. Back in London, beginning in 1561, Bodley was granted a patent for the exclusive printing of the Geneva Bible. In 1565 or 1566, Archbishop Parker and Bishop Grindal recommended that the grant be extended for another twelve years, though still subject to implied conditions that Bodley's son, Thomas, could not accept. Thomas had taken up his father's publishing work in 1563.[88]

William Cole is mentioned in the *Livre des Anglois* as having been in Geneva by 5 June 1557. He married Jane Agar while there. He appeared in Zurich in April of 1554 and was in Frankfurt in the autumn of 1556. He may have spent the winter of 1556–57 with John Foxe and John Bale in Basel. While in Zurich, Cole signed the letter written on 13 October 1554 in answer to Whittingham's letter from Frankfurt.[89]

Another Cole is mentioned in the *Troubles at Frankfort*, Thomas Cole, and there is genuine confusion between William Cole and Thomas Cole in the literature. Christina Garrett believed that the two Coles were brothers because both were from Lincolnshire. Patrick Collinson knew of a Thomas Cole as a "flagrant nonconformist" who was archdeacon of Essex during Elizabeth's reign. No Thomas Cole is mentioned in the *Livre des Anglois*, however, and very little is known about him. Most of the information about a Cole during the period of the Marian exile has to do with William Cole.[90]

William Cole was admitted to Corpus Christi College on 28 July 1545, finishing his B.A. in 1548 and M.A. in 1552. While in Oxford, he was in the company of Peter Martyr Vermigli and Rudolph Gualter, the latter a special mentor to Cole. We have several letters of Cole although they deal mainly with private matters.[91] Little is known of Cole's activities until 1568 when he became president of Corpus Christi College, Oxford. His appointment as president was exceedingly stormy because of his Marian exile and association with the "Zurichian discipline." Elizabeth had wanted Cole as president of Corpus Christi in spite of local opposition, and Robert Horn, Bishop of Winchester, was sent to look into the situation and to discern what the problems were. He and his colleagues, however, were not even allowed to enter the gate of the college. They were eventually admitted only to find that a minority had elected Cole as president. Sometime later, Elizabeth commissioned Horn, Cecil, Thomas Cooper,

Humphrey and George Ackworth to visit Corpus Christi and get the college to shape up for the Protestant cause with support for Cole.[92]

Cole turned out to be a poor president. The college became heavily in debt, and other complaints about Cole's administration forced Horn to depose him. Upon hearing the news, Cole emotionally responded, "Why, my good Lord, must I then eat mice at Zurich again?" Horn was left without retort and allowed Cole to remain with the college. He eventually resigned, however, and became dean of London.

But why had Cole been the Queen's choice? Robert Dudley, the Earl of Leicester, was chancellor of the university, and was influential in getting Cole the nod. Horn wrote to Parker, a letter the Archbishop shared with Grindal, to inform him of the situation at Corpus Christi, and this was the likely impetus for the visitation to the college which resulted in support of Cole.[93]

William Cole had been one of the last of the Geneva exiles to leave the city in 1560. He doubtless saw the Geneva Bible to its completion. His hand may have been in the project from its inception. Upon his return to England, he had livings at Heyford and Salisbury, Winchester and Lincoln, ultimately becoming dean of the latter. Collinson mentions his preaching to merchant adventurers in Antwerp in 1564 under Grindal.[94]

But what may be concluded from this checkered portrait? Cole wrote nothing of record except one curious German tract from Geneva in 1559 which was sent to John Bale in Basel. The brief tract was a commentary or journal concerning the developments of the reformation in Scotland, obviously information Cole gleaned from Knox in Geneva. The names of Coverdale and Bullinger are prominent in the piece as if this would be important information to Bale.[95] One might surmise that Cole was not an original thinker or theologian but a good friend of his fellow refugees, a loyal follower of the Marian exile agenda, especially in its Geneva form, and an arch-supporter of the puritan cause during the time of Elizabeth. That he found himself in the company of greater and more spirited men made his own career less than either great or spirited by comparison.

Robert Field is mentioned in the *Livre des Anglois*, along with his wife Rose, in the company of the Geneva church on 26 November 1557. Field became registered as a resident on 29 November the same year. Little is known of Field. We know of a Robert Fills who translated the *Lawes and Statutes of Geneva* from French in 1562, and the *Dictionary of National Biography* attributes the project to Field, as well as a translation of Beza's *A brief and pithie Summe of the*

Christian faith. The confusion is further apparent in a letter of Thomas Wood to Whittingham in which Wood mentioned that "Fitz" had translated "Mr. Beza's Confessions in English," and that although these were being burned in the Stationers Hall in London, "Fitz" had vouchsafed that his translation was faithful to the French. Was this "Fitz" the Richard Fitz of the separate London churches or Robert Field the Geneva exile? Garrett, in her typically tantalizing way, speculates that Robert Field was the father of John Field, head of the classis movement in London and co-author of the *Admonition to Parliament* in 1572.[96] How plausible might it be that Field, Fills and Fitz are the same person?

The *Lawes and Statutes of Geneva* was dedicated to the friend of puritans, Lord Robert Dudley, the Earl of Leicester, with the recommendation that the laws of Geneva were "without which no common wealth can be ruled." Ecclesiastical discipline was important in Geneva and England would do well to emulate the Genevan pattern. The author seemed especially sensitive to the criticism of the Geneva refugees that they were living lives of luxury abroad, i.e. in "liberty and licentiousness most unlusty."[97] No, indeed, the English did not "enjoy more unchastened freedom of sensual life" while they were exiled on the Continent; in fact, their deportment and demeanor were all the more scrutinized by the ecclesiastical discipline that the author commended to his motherland.

A briefe and pithie Summe of Christian faith, translated from Beza's French edition in 1589, was dedicated to the Earl of Huntington, another puritan patron. The translator, "R. F.," suggested that he was known personally to the Earl. In the preface, the translator noted that there was a dearth of preaching in England, "most specially in the cathedral churches." A strong Deuteronomic view of history is noteworthy, for the translator was convinced that there was a lack of discipline in England, and that unless it was administered at the government level, England's ongoing problems with France would continue to bring God's wrath.[98]

Fills (or Field) has also been credited with translating *Godly Prayers and Meditations paraphrasticallye made upon all the Psalms* in 1577, which later assumed the title of *The Anatomie of the Soule* in 1590. It was dedicated to "the Right Honorable my verye good Lord, the Lord Ferie, L. Vycount Herff. & c.," who was likened to king Josiah because he "restored the law of the Lord to the Israelites, and manfully advanced and defended the same." The translator believed that the psalms of David were some of the most inspirational parts of the Bible because they spoke to believers in the hour of their trials and vicissitudes; in fact the reflections of the psalmist were an expression of the "anatomy of the soul." The tenor of the piece is similar to the spirit and theological tradition of the annotations of the 1560 Geneva Bible.[99]

Yet another translation by Fills (Field) was published from London. *A treatise conteining certain meditations of trew and perfect consolation* was dedicated to Robert Dudley. Fills wrote in the preface that he was reading during a time of persecution and came across this French piece. What "a time of persecution" refers to is not clear from the preface, but Fills may have referred to his time of difficulty during the Marian exile. He contrasted this difficult time with the tranquillity and prosperity of the current queen's reign, surely Elizabeth's, but Fills also noted the insecurity and contempt experienced by many of God's ministers. Their lot would be better with fairer stipends and reasonable livings, but "those who are not resident with their flock should be deprived." The Church of England is not what it ought to be, but there is no comparing it to the time "when we (ye) sang mass" during the days the papists were in power.[100]

But whose sentiments were these? The identity of the Robert Field, exile in Geneva, remains fairly unknown, and whether he can be identified with Robert Fills the prolific translator of Protestant books and pamphlets can remain only a conjecture. It is still intriguing, nevertheless, to titillate the imagination with Field, Fills and Fitz being the same person!

One remaining name listed in the *Livre des Anglois* deserves recognition. **John Baron** was entered among the residents of Geneva on 14 October 1557, designated "student" from Edinburgh. He was accepted as burgher on 21 June 1558. He remained with the last of the English refugees and was one of several noteworthy members of the church to submit the *Livre des Anglois* to the city. He did not leave Geneva until after March of 1560, and doubtless had important work to contribute toward the completion of the Geneva Bible. Along with Whittingham, Baron was responsible for the publication of Knox's treatise on predestination which was also printed at Geneva.[101]

Baron was first seen on the Continent at Basel where in the register of the Church of St. Theodore his son was baptized on 8 January 1554. Baron had married an English woman, Anne Goodacre, and their daughter, Susan, was born while they were in Geneva; the child died in 1558. On his return to Scotland, Baron became minister of Galston in Ayrshire. His wife ran away and took refuge in York. In order to get Anne back, Baron made an appeal to the Grand Assembly of Scotland; Knox helped him with the appeal. When the appeal reached Archbishop Parker, he seemed indifferent. Perhaps he was chagrined to be helping someone of Knox's acquaintance since the Archbishop loathed the political theology of the Knox-Goodman school and much of the radical puritanism associated with Geneva. Parker suggested that he did not want to set an undesirable precedent, and Anne Goodacre Baron remained in England. In February of 1567, John Baron was transferred to Whitehorn in Galloway.[102]

In 1562, Baron published *Ane Answer made the fourth day of septembre a thousand fyue hundreth syxtie & one, by maister Theodore de Beza*. The piece was appended by another of Beza's answers, "the 26 day of the said month unto certein articles of replie set forth by the said cardinell" (the Cardinal of Lorraine). In the preface, Baron wrote that he had known Beza as a learned man deserving of having these tracts translated into English. Because of the influence of Romanism, the tracts should be made available in order to rebuke false teaching. Beza had especially addressed the nature of the church and the marks whereby the true church can be known. Using Augustine, Beza called the church those "called" by God, invisible to the human eye and known only to God. The church includes both wheat and chaff, thus it is necessary to be able to identify it in its true form by its visible marks, proclamation of the word of God and sincere administration of the sacraments. Beza admitted that some reformers had added ecclesiastical discipline as a third mark, but his position was that the third mark was unnecessary because sin can prevent the recognition of the first two marks. Beza's ecclesiology included the necessity of pastors and doctors as ministries within the church; these are not to be subject to apostolic succession as the Romanists believe and practice, for the only true apostolic succession should be a succession of doctrine not of persons. The church is the locus of God's salvation in Christ, but even as the body of Christ, she may err; one cannot accept the infallibility of her councils throughout Christian history.

The evidence of Beza's appeal, Baron pointed out emphatically, was the scriptures. Tradition and church history cannot be placed on the same level as par with Holy Writ. Once this fundamental difference between Protestantism and Catholicism is recognized, church fathers such as Augustine, whom Beza believed to have recognized the authority of the Bible over tradition, can be appealed to and read with great profit. Sensitive to Augustine's statement that the church had preceded scripture, Beza replied that he spoke thus as a Manichean which both he and Jerome would later correct.[103]

Baron's translation of Beza's tracts epitomized the life of a little known Scot who spent time in Geneva during Mary Tudor's reign. He learned in what a fellow Scot would call "the most perfect school of Christ" not only about his own Protestantism, but much more: a reformation in need of constant vigilance and duty, careful not to acquiesce to the fleshpots of Egypt in the form of Romanisms which abrogated the pattern of pure apostolic Christianity as found in the Bible.

IV. JOHN KNOX'S GENEVA CAREER

John Knox, the renown Scottish reformer, clearly was one of the most important and controversial figures during the Marian exile. On 2 January 1553, he had been sent to Buckinghamshire as a Protestant preacher. Edward VI was very ill and would soon die, and Knox returned to Newcastle the following December. He fled to Dieppe, for he was abroad sometime in January 1554, probably the result of illegal arrangements with Protestant seamen. He left Dieppe at the end of February and journeyed through France and Switzerland where he met Calvin for the first time. Calvin gave him a letter of introduction to Bullinger. Knox returned to Dieppe from which he sent letters to his erstwhile parishioners in England on the 10th and 31st of May. He was back in Geneva the following summer where he remained until November when he accepted the call to become minister of the English church at Frankfurt.[104]

The events of 1554, as we have observed, were critical for the Scot. He had by this time developed the theory that Protestant subjects of a Catholic sovereign could lawfully overthrow their magistrate by armed rebellion although he had not worked out the theory systematically. Knox affirmed that he had tested the theory with Calvin, and not long after had addressed the famous four questions concerning resistance of an ungodly magistrate to Bullinger at Zurich. Calvin's response to Knox's theory was the denial of any legitimate circumstances of civil resistance with the use of force. Bullinger's answers to Knox's questions allowed for more ambiguity.[105]

Knox had gone to Zurich with Calvin's letter of introduction, but he stayed only a short spell. He returned to Dieppe, as we have noted, from which he wrote *An Epistle to his afflicted Brethren in England* together with *Exposition of the Sixth Psalm* on 10 May 1554. Three weeks later he wrote *A Comfortable Epistle sent to the afflicted church of Christ, exhorting them to bear his cross with Patience*, in which he advised the Protestants to restrain from using violence. In July of that same year, two more of Knox's pamphlets were published illegally with publication locations falsified: *Letter to the Faithful in London, Newcastle and Berwick*, issued with his *Confession and Declaration of Prayers*, and the famous *A Faithful Admonition, made by John Knox unto the Professors of God's Truth in England.* He remained in Dieppe for two or three months before returning to Geneva. His stated desire was to study with Calvin, to learn Greek and Hebrew, and to gain a better knowledge of Calvin's theology. But because of the invitation to join the Frankfurt refugee church as minister, his studies would have to wait for a season.[106]

Five turbulent months later, Whittingham, Gilby, Goodman and others joined Knox at Geneva to take advantage of Calvin's invitation to establish an English refugee church. Meanwhile, Knox had written his own account of the "troubles at Frankfurt" accusing Cox, Bale, Turner and Jewell of demeaning him before the city council of Frankfurt. His account is not decidedly invective, but he had special words for Thomas Lever whose demeanor Knox considered unchristian. Ironically Lever would spend some time in Geneva prior to the establishment of the English church. After Calvin had reprimanded the Cox group at Frankfurt, they replied with their only account of the Frankfurt fracas. Defending their deportment and the Edwardian Prayerbook, they wrote that they found Knox's political views too radical and at least partially responsible for the Marian persecutions in England.[107]

After four months in Geneva with the English church, Knox was summoned back to Scotland. Correspondence with his mother-in-law during his stay in Geneva motivated him to leave for Edinburgh in September 1555. He would stay until sometime the next year. Before he left, he drew up detailed instructions on how the Protestant services should be carried out during his absence. He provided these in his 7 July 1556 letter, "A Letter of Wholesome Counsel addressed to his Brethren in Scotland." The bishops in Scotland became alarmed at the success of Knox's preaching and called him to appear at the Blackfriars Kirk in Edinburgh on 15 May 1556. Knox appeared escorted by John Erskine of Dun and other sympathizers. The meeting was strangely suspended and Knox preached on the day of the summons to his largest audience ever in Edinburgh.[108]

He returned to Geneva with his wife, Marjorie, and her mother. After his arrival, the same proceedings were renewed against him by Scottish officials, but now that he was in Geneva he could not answer the summons in person. Knox would later report that he was condemned and excommunicated by the provincial council and that his effigy was burned at the cross of Edinburgh.[109] He and his family were formally admitted to the English church on 13 September 1556, and Knox was elected minister the following December along with Christopher Goodman; they would serve as co-pastors for the next year. In May of 1557, Scots arrived in Geneva bearing a letter which requested his imminent return to Scotland. He consulted with Calvin and decided to go back to Scotland, although he would not leave for four months. He was afraid of civil war in Scotland, and he had just witnessed the birth of his son, Nathaniel.[110]

On 24 October 1557, Knox reached Dieppe only to be delivered a letter which advised him against returning to Scotland. He was annoyed, and wrote Glencairn and others in such a mood: he had traveled eight-hundred miles to Dieppe and was miffed that the Scottish nobility had not exerted more resolution. He interpreted their inaction as support of the French reducing them to mere French serfs. When his letter went unanswered he concluded that the reformation in Scotland was being used as a political ploy for selfish gain. He expressed such sentiments in a follow-up letter on 17 December 1557. While in Dieppe he wrote yet another letter back to Scotland and an *Apology for the Protestants holden in Prison in Paris*, as well as a pamphlet that was never published but which supported the Huguenots in Paris.[111]

Before the winter of 1558, he was back in Geneva where he would stay uninterrupted for nearly a year and produce no less than six books and pamphlets as co-pastor of the English church. Jasper Ridley, one of Knox's many biographers, says that "one of these created a greater uproar than anything that had been published in Europe since Luther's three great treatises."[112] This was the *First Blast of the Trumpet against the Monstrovs Regiment of Women*. In the summer of 1558, he wrote and published three additional tracts, each appealing to the Scottish bishops to revoke the sentence of his condemnation. One was addressed to Mary of Lorraine, one to the nobility and parliament, and one to the common people of Scotland. His letter to the queen-regent was a revision of a 1556 letter although quite harsher in tone. His *Letter to the Commonality of Scotland* was published with the *Appellation to the Nobility and Estates of Scotland* under Knox's own name at Geneva. It contained also Gilby's *Admonition to England and Scotland* and a revolutionary poem based on the ninety-fourth Psalm by William Kethe. The remainder of the collection was a short note acknowledging his authorship of the *First Blast* and a brief summary of a proposed "Second Blast."[113]

Calvin and Geneva were appalled. Both Knox and Goodman had been made citizens of Geneva, and Goodman had recently put his controversial sermon into book-form in *How Svperior Powers Oght to be Obeyd*. Exiles in Strasburg, especially Sir Anthony Cooke, complained and sent a letter to Beza which was forwarded to Calvin. Calvin responded that he did not agree with the political theology of the co-pastors of the English church and that measures had been taken to ban the sale of their books.[114] Francis Hotman, propagandist of the French Protestants in Strasburg, condemned Knox, although sixteen years later he would affirm some of the same arguments against Catherine de Medici. Knox wrote to Foxe defending the *First Blast*, doubtless because he had heard of the martyrologist's strong objection to it.[115]

But it was Elizabeth who raised the biggest furor over such propaganda. She ordered Cecil to write to Calvin, but Calvin's response to the Elizabethans was that the books had been published without his knowledge.[116] Another Strasburg exile, John Aylmer, answered Knox in April of 1559 in *Harbor for Faithful True Subjects against the late blown Blast*, in which Knox was accused of taking a particular case and arguing fallaciously to a general conclusion. In reality, Knox's blast had been blown out of season! But the overriding reality was that Knox's book forged a huge chasm between him (and his Geneva cohorts) and the Queen, and she never forgave him. Her main objection was not so much the book's anti-feminism, though distasteful enough, but its revolutionary, tyrannicidal character.[117]

Knox wrote another important tract during the last half of 1558 although it was not published until 1560. The delay was due to the storm caused by the *First Blast*. On 9 November 1559 the censor of books in Geneva reported that Knox's new book had nothing objectionable in it, and that the book could be authorized for publication if the name of Geneva were absent and if Whittingham and John Baron would be responsible for it. Nothing contrary to "catholic and orthodox" doctrine was to be appear in the book. Ridley's comment is worthwhile:

> It is an irony that the only book that Knox ever wrote against men more radical than himself, and that defended the Calvinist doctrine against Calvin's opponents and justified the actions of the government of Geneva against their critics, should have aroused more suspicions in Geneva than anything else that he published there.[118]

The title was *Answer to a Great Number of Blasphemous Cavillations*. It was Knox's longest book, a treatise on many themes which defended the Reformed theology against Anabaptists and Freewillers in general and the Libertine Party in Geneva, Münzer and the revolutionaries in the Peasants' Revolt in particular. The book was a response to an anonymous Anabaptist tract, *The Confutation of the Errors of the careless by Necessity*, written by an English Anabaptist.[119]

A few months later Knox would return to Scotland to join in the revolution against Catholicism. Glencairn, Lord James and Erskine of Dun, in a letter written in November 1558, had urged him to return. Calvin received one at the same time urging him to encourage the Scot to return to his native land.

Yet it was six months before Knox left Geneva. Marjorie was giving birth to their second child, Eleazer, Coverdale having been named as the child's godfather. Knox and Goodman had been elected as ministers again to serve for the coming year. Knox still had his mind on England, for on 10 November he wrote a pamphlet in the form of a letter to the people of England, especially his former congregations at Berwick and Newcastle, many of whom he believed to have acquiesced under Marian pressure. Unknown to Knox, however, was that Mary was on her deathbed, and before the letter would arrive, Elizabeth would be crowned queen.[120]

On 12 January 1559, Knox completed *A Brief Exhortation to England for the Speedy Embracing of Christ's Gospel* and published it with *Epistle to the Inhabitants of Newcastle and Berwick* at Geneva later the same year. About this time a letter was drafted by all the Geneva exiles and sent by William Kethe to the other refugee congregations in exile. It was a conciliatory effort to renew friendship and a sense of brotherhood, and to patch old wounds with the news that England had a Protestant queen. Frankfurt answered favorably, but hedged at the repairing of factions for the future, for all such questions about ceremonies and church order would of necessity need to await the Queen's new policies. But most of the refugees were in a conciliatory mood and optimistic that things had turned for the better now that Mary was no longer on the throne.

Knox finally left Geneva on 28 January 1559. He left his wife, his children, all born in Geneva, and Mrs. Bowes behind; they would join him at safer times. He arrived at Dieppe where he took part in an eventful mass conversion of French Catholics and performed ministerial functions for six or seven weeks for the new Protestant converts. Elizabeth refused him permission to visit England enroute to Scotland, and it is no surprise that the Scot's attacks on Elizabeth's via media became more embittered, his special target the prayerbook. He confessed to Cecil that being rebuffed by the Queen was no loss to him, but that he was indeed shocked by her pettiness in refusing him license to return to England. After all, he chided Cecil, God had spared the Secretary's life notwithstanding his apostasy during the reign of Mary! He knew that the problem was "my book" but he avowed authorship of it and no one else should be blamed or held accountable. Knowledgeable readers were able to find nothing treasonable in it, and if Elizabeth would only stop to reflect on his ideas surely she would be of the same mind; indeed, the two of them could agree that there are exceptions to certain general policy, and like Deborah of old, the Queen could well be an exception.[121] Ridley is correct to suggest that Elizabeth and Knox agreed on two salient points: first, that women should be subject to men; and second, that she was an exception to the rule. Where they differed was on the issue of why the Queen was an exception. For Elizabeth, it was the sole reason that she was queen; for the Scot, it was because she was Protestant. The issue was penetrating, even prophetic. The Queen believed that she should be obeyed in trust by her subjects in whatever she ordered. Knox saw things otherwise. She should be obeyed as long as she was the right kind of Protestant. In the difference lay the nexus to much of the puritan dynamic within the English Reformation.[122]

Knox left Dieppe by boat and arrived at Leith on 2 May 1559, his greatest hour yet to come.

V. ANNE LOCKE

One of Knox's closest associates in Geneva had been Anne Locke. Anne (Prowse) was the daughter of Stephen Vaughn, a merchant with Protestant disposition who had urged Cromwell to intervene on behalf of Tyndale when he was arrested in 1535. Vaughn died in 1549–50, and sometime later within the next six years, Anne married Henry Locke, a mercer from a long line of mercers. Thomas Wood had some dealings with Henry Locke before the former's departure for Frankfurt in 1554, since he too was a mercer. Locke seems to have been Protestant in a sense quite different from his wife although they made quite a cultured family.

Knox wrote thirteen letters to Anne Locke (which have survived) from 1556 to 1562. The first letters were written from Geneva to London to encourage her to come to Geneva. In his letter of 9 December 1556, we have the reference to Geneva as "the moist perfyt schoole of Chryst that ever was in the erth since the dayis of the Apostillis." Knox had stayed with the Locke family in the later months of 1553 before his departure for the Continent. Robert Louis Stevenson would later write a little-known essay entitled, "John Knox and his Relations to Women," in which he expressed his belief that Locke was the woman Knox truly loved the most. As a result of Knox's urging Anne Locke went to Geneva arriving on 8 May 1557 with her son, Harry, and a daughter, Anne. The *Livre des Anglois* recorded that the daughter died in Geneva. Her husband is named

Harry in the record left by the English, but Collinson contends that Locke had deserted her husband during Mary's reign. Locke is depicted "as a widow who might almost be described as a female elder or deaconess." While in Geneva she translated Calvin's sermons on the Song of Hezekiah from Isaiah 38. The sermons were followed by *A meditation of a penitent sinner*, a metrical paraphrase of the fifty-first Psalm. Many of Knox's letters back to Geneva were addressed to her, for Knox relied upon Locke to deliver news about the events in Scotland to other members of the Geneva congregation often with specific messages to Goodman, Coverdale and John Bodley. She left Geneva for Frankfurt in late March and was back in England by the summer of 1559. Henry died in 1571, and Anne was later married to the puritan, Edward Dering, "a successor, surely to Knox rather than to Henry Locke."[123]

In November of 1559, Knox had asked Locke to send Calvin's latest works, including the recent edition of the *Institutes*, and to encourage financial support for the Protestant army in Scotland. We do not hear of Locke for some ten years after this. It is assumed that she held a commanding and respected position among London puritans.[124] Dering died on 26 June 1576 at the age of thirty-six amidst a turbulent time for puritans in London.

Anne married Richard Prowse sometime before 1583. He became a member of Parliament in 1584. He had been an Exeter draper and a substantial figure in West Country affairs. As we have seen, Christopher Goodman preached a controversial sermon in Exeter in 1583, and his visit was likely welcomed by Anne and Richard.

In January of 1583 John Field published part of a minor work on the temptation of Christ which Knox had sent Locke in 1556; it was dedicated to Mrs. Prowse as a form of compensation for not asking her permission. Field asked to receive any other writings of the Scottish reformer, and Anne was probably the resource of Knox's letters coming into the possession of Andrew Melville and other Scots who were exiled in England in 1584–85. Field also collected Edward Dering's writings and, as he told Locke, had plans to edit them. The collected *Workes* of Dering as we have them in the 1597 edition can therefore be credited in part to Anne Locke.

In 1590, Locke translated into English the French work of Jean Taffin, *Of the markes of the children of God, and their comfort in affliction*, which targeted the sufferings of Dutch Protestants but which Anne believed would be especially helpful soon in England because of troublesome days ahead. The better days of "Gospel liberty under Elizabeth are already passing," she wrote. Little wonder that

Collinson suggests that "Anne Locke's life spans the whole story of the Reformation in England...."[125]

NOTES

[1]Garrett suggests his arrival date as 7 April 1556; see Garrett, pp. 250–51.

[2]Knappen, p. 165.

[3]His treatise was *Tractatus de praedestinatione;* see *Works of James Pilkington, Bishop of Durham*, ed. James Scholefleld, Parker Society (Cambridge: University Press, 1842); and, Dewey D. Wallace, *Puritans and Predestination: Grace in English Protestant Theology* (Chapel Hill: University of North Carolina Press, 1982), p. 35.

[4]Cambridge University Library, Baker Mss., Vol. 32, Mm. 1.43, pp. 427–30.

[5]See chapter two. Cf. Richard Bauckham, "Marian Exiles and Cambridge Puritanism: James Pilkington's 'Halfe a Score'," *Journal of Ecclesiastical History* 26 (1975), 137–48; Collinson, *Godly People*, p. 216.

[6] Garrett, pp. 285–86; Mitchell, p. 7. Pollard and Redgrave, *STC*, indicates that the letter was published at Zurich.

[7]Garrett, pp. 285–86; John Strype, *Ecclesiastical Memorials* (Oxford: Clarendon Press, 1822), II.i, 335.

[8]Garrett, pp. 285–86; Foxe, *Acts and Monuments*, VIII, 38.

[9] At Easter of the same year, 1559, he was chosen as one of the disputants on the Protestant side at the Conference of Westminster. See Garrett, pp. 285–86. She has mistakenly given Scory's appointment as Bishop of Hereford on 23 June 1559.

[10]W.A.J. Archbold, *DNB*, XVII, 946–47.

[11]*Two bokes of the noble doctor and B.S. Augustine theone entitled of the Predestination of saints, thother of perserueraunce vnto thende...translated out of Laten into Englishe by John Scory the late B. of Chichester, 1555* [CUL 1556] (10 Calen. Martij), fos. 3, r–7, v; A2, r–v.

[12] Neither Pilkington nor Scory fit in well with N. M. Sutherland's thesis that the exiles presented no unified front to undermine the Elizabethan Settlement, and although both were Elizabethan bishops (Scory had been an Edwardian bishop as well), they wanted to take the reformation much further than allowed by the Queen. See N. M. Sutherland, "The Marian Exiles and the Establishment of the Elizabethan Regime," *Archiv für Reformationsgeschichte* 78 (1987), pp. 253–84. For additional discussion of Sutherland's thesis, see below.

[13] Mitchell, pp. 9, 14; Garrett, pp. 86–87; A. B. Grosart, *DNB*, II, 284.

[14]Strype, *Ecclesiastical Memorials*, III.i, 82; John Rouse Bloxam, *A Register of the Presidents, Fellows, Demies...of Saint Mary Magdalen College* (Oxford: W. Graham, 1853), II, xliii–xliv, IV, 68–74, *passim*.

[15]*Troubles*, pp. 13ff, 97.

[16]Brit. Mus. Harle. Ms. l, p. 237, 416.31, fo. 63; see Strype, *Ecclesiastical Memorials*, III.ii, 132–35. For the nature of these London "exile churches" see Knappen, pp. 152ff.

[17]Foxe, *Acts and Monuments*, VIII, 559–60.

[18]Strype, *Annals*, I.ii, 188.

[19]See his letter to Gilby, 12 November 1565, Cambridge University Library, Baker Mss., Vol. 31, Mm. 1.43, p. 434.

[20]Brook, I, pp. 151–66; see also *The Second Parte of a Register*, I, 68–74, and Collinson, *Elizabethan Puritan Movement*, pp. 67–68, 337, 479. Collinson believes that the conference related by Brook to have taken place in 1570 is "too early," and that the likely date is 1573.

[21]*A notable and comfortable exposition, vpon the fovrth of Mathew, concerning the tentations of Christ, Preached in S. Peters Church, Oxenford.* Thomas Bentham, London (n.d.), fos. B1, v–B2, r; C6, r–v, *passim*. See also Grosart, *DNB*, II, 284, and M. Rosemary O'Day, "Thomas Bentham: A Case Study in the Problems of the Early Elizabethan Episcopate," *Journal of Ecclesiastical History* 23 (1972), 137–59.

[22] J. F. Mozley, *Coverdale and His Bibles* (London: Lutterworth Press, 1953), p. 23. Mozley indicates that the letter was written to Thomas Cole. There is no evidence that Thomas Cole was in Geneva, and the only Cole mentioned in the *Livre des Anglois* is William Cole. The Cole addressed in the letter from Coverdale was likely William Cole.

[23]Garrett, pp. 132–34; *Remains of Myles Coverdale*, ed. for the Parker Society by George Pearson (Cambridge: University Press, 1846), p. 504. Martin gives too much credit to Coverdale in the composition of the Geneva Bible, and Garrett, strictly following Martin, perpetuates this misappropriation. Cf. Martin, pp. 76–78, 230.

[24]Mozley, p. 9.

[25]*Ibid.*, pp. 14–17.

[26]Foxe, *Acts and Monuments*, VI, 705ff. H. R. Tedder, *DNB*, IV, 1289–97, conjectures that one of the servants was Coverdale's wife, but Mozley believes his wife would have accompanied him because of her Danish ties as a generally understood or customary exigency. See Mozley, p. 20.

[27]See *Remains of Myles Coverdale*, vii–xxiii, and *Writings and Translations of Myles Coverdale*, ed. for the Parker Society by George Pearson (Cambridge: University Press, 1844), pp. 425–433.

[28]N. M. Sutherland's study is an attempt to debunk Garrett and Neale who argued that the exiles presented some kind of united front to force Elizabeth to form religious policy more Protestant than she wanted. Sutherland shows that the exiles who were in the Parliament of 1559 "were men who could reasonably be expected by their patrons...to have supported and assisted the government...." In fact, Sutherland argues, there was no "opposition party" to Elizabeth's future settlement of religious policy, for in 1559 "there were no puritans," and "on the leadership level" the exiles may be said to have "played a significant part in assisting the queen to execute the religious settlement." He concludes that the exiles, whom he tends to lump together both geographically and ideologically, were "generally temperate establishment men whose opposition mainly consisted in getting away with local deviations." As such, they were the

architects of Anglicanism. See N. M. Sutherland, "The Marian Exiles...." After examining the activity of the English exiles of Geneva, and the part, albeit small yet clearly influenced by the Genevan ethos, that bishops and future bishops played in that activity, I flnd Sutherland's case unpersuasive, his argumentation somewhat specious, and his presentation in need of the careful nuancing necessary to grasp the many-sidedness of the puritan spectrum in both pre-Elizabethan and Elizabethan times.

[29]Garrett, pp. 279–81; Brook, I, 379–84; Venn and Venn, *Alumni catabrigienses*, Part I, IV, 12; Joseph Foster, *Alumni Oxonienses* (Oxford: J. Parker & Co., 1891), IV, 1307. C. H. Cooper and Thompson Cooper, *Athenae Cantabrigienses* (Cambridge: Deighton, et.al., 1861), II, 43, doubt that Sampson was admitted to study St. Paul's epistles at Oxford, but cf. Anthony Wood, *Athenae Oxonienses*, I, 548. Garrett has a difficult time following Sampson's life because she postulates two men of that name.

[30]Thomas Sampson, *A letter to the trew professors of Christs Gospel/ inhabitinge in the Parish off Allhallowis/ in Bredstrete in London* (Strasburg, 1554). Cf. Richard Bauckham, *Tudor Apocalypse. Sixteenth Century Apocalypticism, Millennarianism and the English Reformation: From John Bale to John Foxe and Thomas Brightman* (Appleford: England: Sutton Courtenay Press, 1978), p. 47.

[31]*Zurich Letters*, III, 176–77. Martin does not believe Sampson had anything to do with the Geneva Bible. There is, however, ample evidence that he remained close to Geneva and corresponded with leaders there; his assistance on the project, especially the text of the Old Testament, should not be disallowed simply on the basis of how long he was a member of the Geneva church. Cf. Martin, p. 242.

[32]*Zurich Letters*, II, 753–55.

[33]*Zurich Letters*, III, 1, 62, 75, 130, 153, 202; see also Collinson, *Godly People*, p. 30.

[34]*Zurich Letters*, Second Series, p. 152.

[35]Brook, I, 375–84.

[36]See Knappen, pp. 187ff; Collinson, *Elizabethan Puritan Movement*, pp. 65ff; cf. Haugaard, *Elizabeth and the English Reformation, passim.*

[37]Strype, *Parker*, I, 322–26.

[38]*Ibid.*, I, 326–27.

[39]*Ibid.*, I, 368, 374–83. See also W. P. Haugaard, "The Episcopal Pretensions of Thomas Sampson," *Historical Magazine of the Protestant Episcopal Church* 36 (1967), 383–86.

[40]Brook, I, 375–84. Among some of Sampson's literary productions during these later years, noteworthy are *A Warning to take heede of Fowlers Psalter* (imprinted at London by Thomas Vautrollier for George Bishop, 1578); *A Briefe collection of the Church, and of certayne ceremonies thereof*, London, printed by H. Middleton, 1581; and *Two Notable Sermons, Made by that worthy Martyr of Christ, Master Iohn Bradford: the one of Repentance, and the*

other of the Lords Supper, now newly imprinted, trans. by Thomas Sampson (London, 1599).

[41]Brook, I, 375–84; Strype, *Annals*, I.ii, 149–51; Thompson Cooper, *DNB*, L, 232–33; Brit. Mus. Lansd. Ms. 982.78, fo. 146.

[42] *Zurich Letters*, I, 292.

[43] To take one example, Sampson's idea of the eucharist sounds much less Zwinglian than Gilby and the notes in the Geneva Bible. Consequently he seems closer to Calvin's eucharistic theology than members of the refugee church who stayed longer in Geneva, ironically in a better position to imbibe more of Calvin's ideas. This should warn historians not to equate Calvinism and Puritanism.

[44]In 1554, he told his former congregation that Calvin had said the last word on the subject of edification, and later in his career, Calvin's *Institutes* was all that was needed to determine the true meaning of biblical repentance. See Sampson, *A letter to the trew professors of Christs Gospel/ inhabitinge in the Parish off Allhallowis*, fo. Bv, v, and *A Warning to take heede of Fowlers Psalter*, p. 75.

[45]J. Cathbert Hadden, *DNB*, XI, 73–74, mistakenly suggests that Kethe came to Geneva with Whittingham. See Garrett, pp. 204–05.

[46]Fos. Bi, v–Ci, r.

[47]Strype, *Ecclesiastical Memorials*, III.ii, 98–116.

[48]*Ibid.*, 207–11.

[49]William Kethe, *A Sermon made at Blanford Forum, in the countie of Dorset on Wensday the 17. of Ianury last past at the session holden there, before the honoble and worshippefull of that Shyre...* (London: John Day, 1571), fo. 8, v.

[50]*Ibid.*, fo. 11, v.

[51]Hadden, *DNB*, XI, 73–74.

[52]Laing believes that twelve of Kethe's psalms were adopted in the English Psalter of 1562. See his *Works of John Knox*, IV, 572.

[53]Strype contends that Kethe also wrote in verse against Miles Huggard's *Against the English Protestants*, written in 1555, but no evidence is available to support his contention. See S. R. Maitland, *Essays on Subjects Connected with the Reformation in England* (London: J. Lane, 1899), pp. 82–83.

[54]E. Irving Carlyle, *DNB*, XXI, 175; Mitchell mistakenly thought that Wiburn had the M.A. in hand while in Geneva. See Mitchell, p. 9.

[55]See, e.g. his *A Check or reproofe of M. Howlets vntimely shreeching in her maiesties eares, with an answer to the reasons alleadged in a discourse thereunto annexed, why Catholickes...refuse to goe to church...* (London, 1581), a reply to the Jesuit, Robert Parsons.

[56] Percival Wiburn, *A Check or reproofe of M. Howlets vntimely shreeching in her maiesties eares...*, fo. 51, r–v.

[57]See Collinson, *Elizabethan Puritan Movement*, p. 439, *passim*; Garrett, p. 331.

[58]Carlyle in the *DNB* attributes *The State of the Church of England* to Wiburn, but Sidney Lee, in the entry of John Udall in the *DNB* attributes the piece to Udall. Both Conyers Read, *Bibliography of British History: Tudor Period, 1485–1603* (Oxford: Clarendon Press, 1933), p. 156, and Collinson, *Elizabethan Puritan Movement*, p, 391, show that Udall was the author. Cf. *DNB*, XX, 426.

[59]W. A. Shaw, *DNB*, XVI, 460; Mitchell, p. 12; Garrett, pp. 262–63; Foxe, VII, 738; VIII, 384. John Pullein is often confused with Valerand Poullain, and the *DNB* entry falls prey to the confusion.

[60]Garrett, pp. 262–63.

[61]Shaw, *DNB*, XVI, 460.

[62]See *Select Poetry*, ed. Edward Farr, Parker Society (Cambridge: University Press, 1845), II, 495, and Wood, *Athenae Oxonienses* I, 345.

[63]Garrett, pp. 193–94; Bloxam, 104ff; *Troubles*, p. 16.

[64]Bloxam, p. 117; Strype, *Parker*, I, 368.

[65]See Knappen, pp. 175–77.

[66]*Ibid.*

[67] Cf. the letters from Humphrey to Gilby in the early 1570s with his later, more moderate puritan position. Cambridge University Library, Baker Mss, Vol. 32, Mm. 1.43, pp. 431–32.

[68]Garrett notes that the Bodlein Library contains a manuscript of an unsigned letter whose heading is inscribed, "libri Roberti Beaumont" along with a list of theology books. It is dated 6 March 1557, and Garrett surmises it to be an early appeal from Geneva to Frankfurt for peace between the two English congregations. See Garrett, p. 83.

[69]Alfred Goodwin, *DNB*, II, 68–69.

[70]*Ibid.* The letter was dated 28 November 1564. See Cambridge University Library, Baker Mss., Vol. 31, Mm. 1.42, p. 81.

[71]Cambridge University Library, Baker Mss., Vol. 32, Mm. 1.43, pp. 427–30.

[72]Goodwin, *DNB*, II, 68–69. Cf. Cambridge University Library Mss., Ely Add. 49, fo. 188, v.

[73]Martin, pp. 60–61; *Troubles*, p. 188.

[74]Collinson, "The Authorship of *A Brieffe Discours*...." Cf. Collinson, *Elizabethan Puritan Movement*, p. 152, where Collinson alludes to Fuller's imprisonment based upon another letter from Thomas Wilcox to Gilby on 21 December 1573, Cambridge University Library, Baker Mss., Vol. 32, Mm. 1.43, pp. 441–42.

[75]*The Second Part of a Register*, ed. Albert Peel (Cambridge: University Press, 1915), II, 57.

[76]*Ibid.*, II, 60.

[77]*Ibid.*

[78]*Ibid.*, II, 62.

[79]*Ibid.*, II, 52.

[80]*Ibid.*, II, 54–55.

[81]*Ibid.*, II, 64.

[82]Mitchell contends that two sons were born in Geneva but implies that they were among Bodley's sons who were mentioned in the *Livre des Anglois*. However, the fourth son who was born in Geneva, Zacharie, is the only son designated as having been born in Geneva. The other sons were named Thomas, John and Lawrence. See Mitchell, pp. 9, 13.

[83]Garrett, pp. 92–94.

[84]*Ibid.*

[85]Mitchell, p. 12.

[86]Garrett, pp. 92–94.

[87]Collinson, *Godly People*, pp. 267–72.

[88]A. F. Pollard, *Records of the English Bible, the Documents Relating to the Translation and Publication of the Bible in English, 1525–1611* (London: Oxford University Press, 1911), p. 25. Garrett notes five autographed letters written by Thomas Bodley in 1583–84, and which are preserved in the archives of Geneva. She is incorrect, I think, to suggest that the Bodleys left Geneva in 1560. See *Calendar of the State Papers,* Domestic, 1547–80, p. 166, and Garrett, pp. 92–94.

[89]*Zurich Letters*, II, 752; Garrett, p. 123; *Troubles*, p. 33.

[90]*Troubles*, pp. 94–95; Garrett, p. 123; Collinson, *Elizabethan Puritan Movement,* p. 68; Canon Venables, *DNB*, IV, 730–32.

[91]See *Zurich Letters* for the years 1558–62; British Museum, Fulman Mss., IX, fos. 88–111; Thomas Fowler, *History of Corpus Christi College with Lists of its Members* (Oxford: Oxford Historical Society, 1893), pp. 124–44; Wood, *Athenae Oxonienses*, I, 447; II, 13; III, 430, 660; IV, 270–71, 281.

[92]Fowler, pp. 124–26.

[93]*Ibid.*, pp. 127–29; Strype, *Grindal*, pp. 196–97.

[94]J. F. Mozley, *Coverdale and his Bibles,* p. 316; Collinson, *Elizabethan Puritan Movement*, pp. 67, 366.

[95]The tract was entitled, *Warhafftige zeitung Bom auffgang des Evangelii...* (Geneva, 1559); it can be found in Cambridge University Library, Ms. Hib. 5.55.1. I know of no other citation or reference to this tract by Cole.

[96]Garrett, pp. 152–53; Ronald Bayne, *DNB*, VI, 1304. Martin, p. 278, and Strype, *Annals*, I.i, 552, also identify Field with Fills. The letter is referred to in Collinson, "The Authorship of *A brieffe Discours...*," but curiously Collinson mentions neither Fills nor Field in *Elizabethan Puritan Movement.*

[97]*Lawes and Statutes of Geneva....* Translated out of French into Englishe by Robert Fills (London: Rowland Hall, 1562), fos. iii, r–iv, v.

[98]*A brief and pithie Summe of Christian faithe made in the forme of a confession....* Made by Theod. De Beza. Translated out of French by R.F. (London, 1589), fos. A4, v–A6, r.

[99]*Godly prayers and Meditations, paraphrasticallye made upon all the Psalms*...translated out of the French into Englishe (London, 1577), fos. Aii, v–Av, r.

[100]*A treatise conteining certain meditations of trew and perfect consolation* (London, n.d.), fos. Avii, v–Bii, v.

[101]Martin, p. 44.

[102]Garrett, p. 81.

[103]Fos. Aii, r–Dvi, r., *passim*. Laing, *Works of John Knox*, III, 80; Foxe, II, 1388; Jasper Ridley, *John Knox* (Oxford: Clarendon Press, 1968), p. 165.

[104]Aeneas MacKay, *DNB*, XI, 308–28; W. Stanford Reid, *Trumpeter of God: A Biography of John Knox* (New York: Charles Scribner's Sons, 1974), pp. 105ff.

[105]See Dan G. Danner, "Resistance and the Ungodly Magistrate in the Sixteenth Century: The Marian Exiles," *Journal of the American Academy of Religion* 49 (1981), 471–81; cf. the letter to Bullinger of 3 May 1554 in *Ioannis Calvini Opera,* ed. G. Baum, et. al. (M. Bruhn, 1876), XV, 125.

[106]Ridley, pp. 180–88.

[107]*Ibid.*, pp. 212ff.

[108]Laing, IV, 463–64; cf. John Knox, *History of the Reformation in Scotland,* Laing's text, I, 252ff.

[109]*Ibid.*

[110]*Ibid.*

[111]Ridley, p. 243; Laing, IV, 251; Mitchell, p. 13.

[112]Ridley, pp. 249–61; cf. Knox, Laing's text, I, 254.

[113]Ridley, pp. 264–79. Ridley erroneously attributes Gilby's *Admonition to England and Scotland* to Knox because "Gilby's name was not widely known."

[114]*Zurich Letters*, Sec. Series, p. 131.

[115]Ridley, pp. 282–85. See also Richard L. Greaves, *Theology and Revolution in the Scottish Reformation: Studies in the Thought of John Knox* (Grand Rapids: Christian University Press, 1980), *passim*, and Greaves, "Calvinism, Democracy, and the Political Views of John Knox," *Occasional Papers of the American Society for Reformation Research* (1977), I, 81–92.

[116]Ridley, p. 291.

[117]*Ibid.*, p. 291–92.

[118]*Ibid.*, p. 292.

[119]Ridley suggests that the author was a follower of Sabastian Castello. Some have identified the author as Robert Cooke. See O. T. Hargrave, "The Predestinarian Offensive of the Marian Exiles at Geneva," *Historical Magazine of the Protestant Episcopal Church* 42 (1973), 111–23; cf. Strype, *Ecclesiastical Memorials,* II.i, 70. No copy of the tract is extant. Greaves believes that Knox's treatise which reflects and explicitly defends Calvin's doctrine of predestination was atypical of Knox, and the main reason he wrote it

was to make amends with Calvin for his unpopular political theology. See Greaves, *Theology and Revolution in the Scottish Reformation*, pp. 26–29.

[120]Ridley, p. 515ff; Mitchell, pp. 12–13. Both of Knox's sons had been born in Geneva; both, however, would become Anglicans as Fellows of St. John's College, Cambridge. See H. C. Porter, *Puritanism in Tudor England* (London: Macmillan, 1970), p. 120.

[121]Laing, VI, 15–21.

[122]Ridley, pp. 312–14.

[123]Collinson, *Elizabethan Puritan Movement*, pp, 134, 152; Mitchell, p. 8; cf. Collinson, "Role of Women in the English Reformation Illustrated by the Life and Friendships of Anne Locke," *Studies in Church History*, ed. G. J. Cuming (London: Thomas Nelson and Sons, 1965), II, 258–72. Collinson attributes the metered psalm to Knox, but it likely was the work of Whittingham or Kethe. Strangely, Locke is not mentioned by Garrett.

[124]Collinson's article on Locke referred to above is also in *Godly People*; see especially pp. 281ff. Most of my portrait of Anne Locke is taken from Collinson's seminal study.

[125]Collinson, *Godly People*, p. 287.

CHAPTER 4

THE THEOLOGY OF THE
GENEVA EXILES

The purpose of this chapter is to reflect upon the biographical portrait of the Geneva exiles in order to ascertain their theology. It will be necessary to test their ideas in the context of the historical and theological background of the Protestant Reformation, especially the Reformed or Rhineland tradition. The most obvious points of contact are the thought of Calvin and Beza. The Zurich tradition, represented by Johannes Oecolampadius and Heinrich Bullinger, will have some bearing as well. The exiles' own English Protestant tradition will be an important backdrop to the discussion, for the continuity and discontinuity within this tradition foreshadows the nature of puritan thought and provides a sense of the chronological beginnings of puritanism. The procedure will be to select certain relevant topics that, when given systematic treatment, become a compendium of theological markings or interest-points. In this way, the theology of the Geneva exiles can be highlighted as one, if not the most noteworthy, puritan dynamic within the English Protestant tradition.

I. THE BIBLE

The principle of *sola scriptura* was one of the hallmarks of Protestantism. English Protestants were no exception although there are distinctive features of English Protestant biblical hermeneutics. The puritans emulated Paul's belief that the world and its antinomies were reconciled in Christ. They desired a progressive realization of the life of the church in perfection. The only feasible way to accomplish this was to mandate that all things be done with clear, scriptural warrant. Since the Bible generates its own principles of order, these must be followed. Thus the Bible was a living source of a spiritual transformation; it was not merely a book of static legalism but a source for the upbuilding of the spiritual journey which culminates in a life taken up into the life of Christ which is its true meaning and end. This must take place within a social organism as a part of God's ongoing revelation in history. It was for this reason that the Bible became for puritans like the Geneva exiles the source for a Deuteronomic reading of God's historic dealings with Israel, and since the exiles saw themselves as part of God's newly covenanted nation their theology was a strictly federal theology.[1] Thus the Bible was the criterion which the Christian magistrate was to use in the reformation of society. It was the "pure word of God which alone had sufficient authority, as the expression of the divine will, to destroy the vain traditions of men."[2]

The "word of God" to English reformers generally and the Geneva exiles particularly was the sixty-six canonical books of the Bible. It is true that God has revealed himself within the human heart and the starry heavens, yet because of human infirmities a perfect knowledge of God is impossible from general revelation; God must reveal himself in a special way. This he has done in Jesus Christ who spoke the wisdom of God which was transmitted by the preaching of the apostles, a record of which is in the scriptures. Thus the Bible is God's word which defines good and evil, and helps to distinguish knowledge from ignorance and light from darkness. Before the church undertakes anything, therefore, it must first consult God's word and then immediately execute it. In the preface to the Geneva Bible of 1560, the reader is informed why the compilers were making this edition available: "so you would willingly receive the words of God, earnestly study it and in all your life practice it, that you may now appear indeed to be the people of God."[3]

No one has the authority to exceed the boundaries of the Bible either to add to or take from. Whatever is not commanded by God's word "touching his service...is against his word." There is no true church "but where as the people are taught by Gods pure word." Preachers of the Gospel "open the gates of heaven with the word of God" which is the key Christ promised his apostles, but "where this word is not purely taught, there is neither key, nor authority." Nothing should be taught "which we have not learned by Gods word."[4]

This theme predominates the annotations of the 1560 Geneva Bible. The emphasis is not on hearing but on knowing and understanding the word of God. The word of God had become an apostolic textbook and the measure of all religious thought and activity. As such, the Bible clearly was the law of God.

> The Gospel is the stablishing & accomplishing of the law.... The doctrine of the Law containeth nothing unprofitable or superfluous.... Whosoever transgress the least of the ten commandments in word and example, he shall be cast out of the kingdom of God, except it be pardoned him in Christ.[5]

Although Christ is the end of the law and prophets, the ten commandments, indeed, all the Old Testament, is included with the New Testament as the word of God.

Thus, when the Geneva exiles referred to the visible marks of the true church of Christ, it is important to emphasize that what Luther and Calvin denoted as the proclamation and hearing of the word of God, the exiles nuanced to the Bible in its canonical entirety. Whereas both Luther and Calvin stressed the soteriological implications of *sola scriptura,* the exiles followed a more Erasmian emphasis whereby the Bible became the source of understanding, wisdom and ultimately salvation. Moreover, the exiles lessened the fiduciary aspect of faith in favor of a more intellectual aspect. Thus the Bible was not Luther's "cradle of Christ" or Calvin's "letter warmed by the Spirit" but a book of propositions, precepts and laws to be followed. It contained models or patterns to be emulated. Revelation does not await the interior witness of the Holy Spirit, although the exiles sometimes alluded to this Calvinist notion; revelation awaits the person whom God illuminates to read and understand the Bible with honesty and diligence.

The hermeneutic which underlies the exiles' view of the Bible is describable as primitivist or restitutionist; the biblical model or pattern was to be implemented in their own times. During the Whitgift-Cartwright debate in the early 1570s, the Archbishop charged Cartwright and the puritans with being schismatic resonant with a stream of Christian heresy which went back as far as the Novations and Donatists and culminated with the Anabaptists. Cartwright's answer was that the puritan agenda was not innovation but renovation, a doctrine not new but renewed, "no stranger but born in Zion."[6] "Contraries can only be cured by contraries," and to try and straighten a crooked stick demands bowing it back as far as it was on its bent side. Why, asked Cartwright, would a parent despair watching her child playing with a dangerous knife when by taking away the knife the danger is avoided! Sir Francis Hastings, who studied under Laurence Humphrey at Oxford, told Elizabeth's last parliament that there were various kinds of "puritans," but what England needed, indeed describing himself, was "evangelical puritans" who "insist wholly upon scriptures as upon a sure ground."[7] The puritan imperative was severe: it was precisely and exclusively biblical; little wonder they were ridiculed as "precisians." As Elizabethan bishops were exhorted, "[B]etter it were that the whole world should perish, than one iota of God's truth should be overslipped."[8]

Both Luther and Calvin allowed traditions which were continuous with the church's past as long as no biblical mandate or principle was violated, although Geneva was clearly more restrictive than Wittenberg. The exiles moved a step farther away from Roman Catholicism. Not only were they unwilling to side with the historic church in the event biblical principles were violated, they wanted to duplicate fully the apostolic precedent for their own day. Their position was closer to Zwingli's iconoclastic reform in Zurich than to the Wittenbergers in Germany, and ironically it was closest to the Anabaptist hermeneutic for which the English reformers felt such disdain.[9]

Thus, when Anthony Gilby wrote *A Pleasavnt Dialogve* in 1581 upbraiding his Elizabethan cohorts for their acquiescence in wearing ecclesiastical vestments, one of his key arguments was that vestments are human inventions for which there is no biblical precedent or warrant—Peter and Paul simply did not adorn their preaching with such innovations! Gilby's part in the *Admonition to Parliament* of 1572 echoed the same theme: the church of England was not practicing the marks of the true church according to apostolic pattern. Instead, ministers were made to conform to the Prayerbook "which have many ungodly things in it"; there were no congregational elections of ministers, indeed, there were no elders in the church of England as Paul enjoined the churches of his day; pomp and ceremony, including kneeling and referring to the eucharistic signs as the "body of our Jesus Christ," had taken the place of the simple but effective worship of the early church; and, there was no public ecclesiastical discipline to edify the house of God in England.[10] The puritans would add to their list: marriage should not be accounted a sacrament, the wedding ring should be given up as a Romish innovation, and women should not attend the ceremony bareheaded with "bagpipes and fidlers before them...to disturb the congregation," and with such elaborate dressing of their hair that they "make a May game of marriage."[11] Puritans went so far as to decry the wafer cake used in communion; it too was a Roman innovation foisted upon the simple usage of common bread in the primitive church.

William Whittingham remained a radical puritan once back in England. His 1566 letter, "To my faythfull Brethren now afflycted," continued his polemic against Catholic accretions of pure apostolic Christianity. One could not argue, as the Elizabethans did, that vestments were indifferent, when the way they were being used was still associated with Rome. The church is made up of people called out from the world who should not practice anything not clearly commanded or exemplified in the Bible. True, vestments were not explicitly forbidden in the early church, but that did not make them indifferent or expedient.

> Now if any man would say, that we do this rather of singularity than of conscience, and that we are so addicted to our own manners, that we will not change for the better, he may understand that if our apparel seem not modest and grave as our vocation requireth, neither sufficient to discern us from men of other callings, we refuse not to wear such as shall be thought to the Godly and prudent Magistrates for these uses most decent, so that we may ever keep ourselves pure from the defiled robes of Antichrist, would to God that this sentence of St. Ambrose were well weighed whereas he saith, as the robe setteth forth the Senator, as husbandry, the husbandman so nothing setteth forth a Bishop, but the works of a Bishop....[12]

Curiously, Whittingham seemed to soften his position in the late 1560s and early 1570s. As we have seen, he seemed convinced by Calvin's argument against the puritans: preaching and the ministry of God's flock should not be impeded by scrupulosity against external adiaphora.

This had been the conclusion also of Robert Beaumont who became vice-chancellor of Trinity College, Cambridge. He did not endorse vestments such as the surplice, and was active in getting rid of many Romish "superstitions," but he could not sacrifice the call to preach the Gospel for the sake of his own conscience and scruples. He could wear the surplice without attributing to it anything more than the license to preach. But Gilby and the more radical puritans believed he had compromised what he had once stood for in Geneva and therefore contributed to the adulteration of the apostolic pattern.[13]

Thomas Sampson represents the opposite shift. Before he went to Geneva he was a moderate Protestant who sided with the Cox party at Frankfurt. But as his exile matured he became influenced by the ideology of the Geneva refugee church, among the exile churches the most radical. Once back in England, he demonstrated an adamant opposition to anything which smacked of Rome. Was it simply an extreme anti-Catholicism? The evidence would suggest that it was more, a hermeneutical difference between how moderates such as Beaumont and radicals such as Sampson interpreted the Bible.

Sampson had changed his views about adiaphora or indifferent matters. Before he went to Geneva, it will be recalled that he had written Calvin to indicate that the Frankfurt church had given up many ceremonies considered indifferent out of respect for those who had scruples against them. After his experience with Whittingham, Knox and Gilby at Geneva, he no longer thought of certain Romish ceremonies and desiderata as indeed indifferent, or if they were, that they should be prescribed by Elizabeth and her bishops. Sampson seemed to bother Bullinger and Martyr with constant questions about adiaphora, and he challenged them to get in line and support what Bucer had begun for the English Protestant church in *De Regno Christi.*

By the mid 1560s Sampson got crossways with Parker over the wearing of vestments and other matters considered adiaphora by the Elizabethans. Parker addressed nine questions to Sampson and Humphrey with each being answered by the deprived preachers with extensive documentation from the Bible and the church fathers. Was the surplice inherently evil or bad? It would depend on the context and what might be associated with it in the public mind. Should not the preachers obey those who had authority over them as Paul enjoined? Only when their conscience might not be mitigated by a higher principle. The preachers' answers followed a familiar pattern: no minister of the Gospel should obey a rule or precept which he conscientiously believed was a "patch of papistry" clearly used for "pomp and effect." The early church did not distinguish between clergy and laity, so why was it necessary for her majesty to prescribe and require clerical distinctions in dress when this had been practiced for acculturated ages by a declining, apostatized church which bears no resemblance to the church of the apostles![14]

If these desiderata were truly indifferent, the puritans hammered that they could not be prescribed as desiderata but must be optional for the user or the social group within which the user functioned. The crux of the puritan dissent does not relate to justification by faith but to their biblical hermeneutic: what scripture commanded the Christian must do; what scripture prohibited the Christian must omit. What was neither commanded nor prohibited was indifferent and was permitted within the free course of Christian charity. But adiaphora should not be legislated and were neither necessary for salvation nor binding upon conscience.[15]

Thus many practices considered adiaphora by conformists were ruled out by nonconformists like Sampson and Gilby. The problem, of course, was to discern the difference between an inveterate appreciation for the aesthetic and an iconoclasm which deemed every traditional ceremony as evil and in need of extrication for the purification of a reformed church. Adiaphora should not foster division although dissent should be guaranteed. But this was too unwieldy for Elizabeth and eventually the canons of reason prevailed in the appeal to civil law.[16] What upset the radical puritans was that the national church appealed to civil law rather than the law of God.

Both Oecolampadius and Bullinger had supported the ethos expressed by scrupulous Edwardian Protestants, yet neither would concede to the reductionist position of the Anabaptists. Bullinger had supported John Hooper's rejection of vestments, but the Zurich reformer gave little assistance to puritans during Elizabeth's reign. The strong opposition to Hooper, even from those who agreed with him on the vestiarian issue, was that his position was deemed seditious. Had he been more diplomatic he could have received similar treatment as that given to Sampson; Cranmer allowed Sampson excuse from wearing vestments at his ordination in 1550 for the sake of conscience.[17]

Bullinger was an enigma to Elizabethan puritans. He gave no support to Sampson and Humphrey when they were in trouble because of nonconformity. In fact, he turned the ever-inquisitive Sampson's query of whether ministers might lawfully be removed for nonconformity into a discussion of deserting the ministry. Yet in the 1550s, Bullinger considered vestments a part of the ceremonial law which had been abrogated by Christ's death. Peter Martyr had given implicit support for Sampson when he expressed that he had never worn the surplice in the choir at Oxford. Obviously something had changed for Zurichers, for now they were advising puritans to compromise as long as there was a safeguard for conscience and the opportunity to preach. Perhaps Bullinger did not want the English to look to the Lutherans for mentoring when Zwinglians offered more promise. The irony was that the "dregs of popery," as Bullinger called vestments, were disapproved in Zurich just as they were in Geneva. Did the Zurichers soften their position and mitigate advise to radicals like Sampson when it appeared that Sampson might have been in line for a bishopric?[18]

Because Bullinger was cast as a supporter of the Elizabethan Settlement in the mid-1560s, puritans, whether they had been exiled in Geneva or not, began looking to Geneva. Whitgift prescribed Bullinger's *Decades* as required reading for ministers in the province of Canterbury, but ironically there were some ideas expressed in the *Decades* which were at variance with the Elizabethan church. Because of his support for the Elizabethans, many of the Marian exiles who had spent time in Zurich were confused and Zurich "never regained the influence it enjoyed in the latter days of Edward VI."[19]

The Geneva refugee church reflected a uniquely English Protestant view of the Bible. The Bible was the only standard for doctrine, church polity and piety. It was a divine source in contradistinction with human tradition, and it gave Christians a criterion by which human tradition should be judged. Exiles such as Whittingham, Gilby and many others we have met in this study envisioned themselves as prophets of God calling the national church back to the old paths of apostolic Christianity. If vestments were not worn by Paul, they need not be worn by London or Cambridge preachers. If the wedding ring were a carryover from Roman Catholic days and there was no example of its usage by the early church it should be excluded from the wedding ceremony. If there were scriptural precedents of elders functioning in a presbyterian church polity, why insist on episcopacy, a form closer to Rome but further from Jerusalem and Antioch?

The puritans who were members of the Geneva church attempted to theologize wherever they believed the word of God led them; one often gets the impression that they were unaware of theologizing at all, feeling they merely replicated the ancient order of things. When they returned to the original sources of Christian antiquity, they felt they were building on the surest of foundations.

II. PREDESTINATION, SALVATION AND GOOD WORKS

Predestination was a popular topic for the Geneva exiles. The marginalia of the Geneva Bible reveal a keen interest in predestination, and there were at least three separate treatises on predestination published by Genevan printers during the English exiles' sojourn in Geneva. James Pilkington, later Bishop of Durham under Elizabeth, had written a treatise on predestination while a student at Cambridge. He stayed for a brief time in Geneva in 1556, the same year that Gilby published his treatise and Whittingham translated Beza's treatise on election, the only section of *Summa totius Christianismi* Whittingham was interested in translating into English. Knox's *Answer to a Great Number of Blasphemous Cavillations* was published in 1560, although he had written the lengthy treatise sometime in 1558. John Scory also had indicated an interest in predestination with his translation of Augustine's writings in 1555.

One surprising note should be sounded at the outset: the exiles did not seem to be too interested in Calvin's predestinarian theology. Both Gilby and Whittingham, for example, appeal to Beza's thought. Gilby's *Treatise on Election* mentions Beza's treatise without any reference to Calvin, and why Whittingham decided to focus on Beza's predestinarian ideas rather than Calvin's remains a bit of a mystery.

The exception was the Scot. In Knox's treatise Calvin's predestinarian theology is given explicit defense. But as we have suggested, Knox seemed somewhat out of character in this piece for he nowhere else seemed to be interested in predestination, certainly not to the degree that he was interested in political theology. It has been conjectured that he may have echoed Calvin's more biblical and systematic theological thrust in order to assuage the Genevan's animosity toward him for writing the *First Blast.*[20]

Calvin's predestinarian ideas had gone through a natural progression which, according to R. T. Kendall, clouded God's election in mystery and hiddenness.[21] The 1559 *Institutes* had placed the doctrine of predestination within the context of salvation rather than the doctrine of God which had characterized the earlier editions, and there is little, if any, scholastic tendency in Calvin's treatment; his chief concern seemed to be the biblical and christological underpinnings of predestination. Nevertheless, Calvin had begun with the 1559 *Institutes* a more explicit elucidation of God's decree against the reprobate.[22] This new emphasis on the "double decree" of predestination was likely the result of Calvin's sharpening his thought as he defended the doctrine against the likes of Sebastian Castellio.[23]

It was Theodore Beza who opened the door for a different emphasis. Beza's notion of a limited atonement went beyond Calvin who believed that Christ had died for all.[24] Although no scholastic, Beza's emphasis on reason and the use of Aristotle and Aquinas laid the groundwork for Protestant scholasticism among later Calvinists.[25] The exiles in Geneva were closer to Beza in their predestinarian theology. Beza and the Heidelberg theologians became the architects of a tradition which included the notions of a limited atonement and a voluntarism that virtually bound God to accept good works as natural concomitants to faith. This surely resonates with the thought of Gilby, whose methodology and argumentation approximate Beza's predestinarian thought in Whittingham's translation of *A Brief declaration of the chiefe poyntes of Christian Religion.* This English exile tradition, coupled as a coalition with Beza's departure from his mentor, Calvin, became the bridge to a later form of English Calvinism represented by William Perkins and the Westminster Confession, hence heir to Beza rather than to Calvin.[26]

The *Brief declaration* showed that the hub or center of Beza's thought was the sovereignty of God (Calvin's earlier position). From everlasting "God hath proposed and decreed...to create all things at their seasons to his glory." From the very beginning, therefore, even logically prior to the decree to create, God had created humankind in two sorts: one to save in order to show mercy, the other to condemn in order to show his wrath toward sin. The former did nothing to merit God's mercy, the latter did everything to merit his wrath, "that he might find matter of just damnation in those, unto whom it is given neither to believe, neither yet to know the mysteries or secrets of God."

Throughout Beza's treatise, the author mentions that God's decree(s) is not based upon divine foreknowledge; what is at the heart of the decree, ontologically, is the inscrutable will of God. God is the author of all things, but not the author of sin; sin was necessary to decree the condemnation of the reprobate, in all equity, because of their own sin. God thus leaves them to sin and does not give them the faith that he gives to the elect. Faith comes from preaching the Gospel and is accompanied by the inward power of the Holy Spirit which does not renew the remnants of free will "as Sophisters do suppose," but rather "turneth their hearts" and opens "their sense, heart, ears and understanding." The Spirit of God thus creates faith in the elect and brings them to a knowledge of their election in Christ, "so that they begin to will and to do the things which are of God."[27]

Can the reprobate hear the Gospel? Yes, some do hear but cannot believe because it has not been given to them. Some even hear as do demons but fall away albeit of their own accord. Some are not even granted the favor of hearing the Gospel. All this scenario is necessary to uphold the sovereignty of an ineffable, inscrutable God, although the reprobate are in no sense compelled.[28]

Faith then is God's gift which allows his Spirit to work within the hearts of the elect, softening, drawing, teaching, enlightening and opening. Faith continues toward sanctification, for the Holy Spirit inspires the elect to perform good works. We continue to sin, but there has been a change in the will, a bewailing of our condition and the desire to amend as a consequence of grace. Christians are initiated into faith by the sacrament of baptism and faith is sealed by the sacrament of the Lord's Supper. Thus Christians may not lose faith for "they still have the seeds of the love of God and neighbor within them."[29]

Beza was convinced that it was not within human power to identify the elect or the reprobate, but when visiting the sick it might be of comfort to assure them of their election, or by pointing out the evils of the reprobate they may be struck by God's severe judgment of sin! The real test of election, however, can be known only from within:

...And when thou hearest the voice of God sounding in thine ears and mind, which calleth thee unto Christ the only mediator, consider by little and little, and search diligently...whether thou be justified and sanctified, that is, made righteous and holy, by faith in Christ, for these are the effects by the which, faith, the very cause of them indeed is known. And this thou shalt know...partly by the spirit of adoption crying within...: partly also by the power and working of the same spirit in thyself: namely if thou feel, and also indeed shew, that although sin do swell in thee, it doth not reign in thee.[30]

Anthony Gilby knew of Beza's work, and was quite willing to let it stand as the last word on the subject of predestination, but since he had already written a treatise himself on the same subject, he felt constrained to polish and revise it for publication in the same year, 1556, which had seen Whittingham's translation of Beza's treatise. "In fact Gilby's work may well have been the earliest original statement of the Calvinist doctrine of predestination to come from an English pen."[31]

Gilby was convinced that the doctrine of predestination precluded despair. God's eternal election showed his majesty and glory, and the scriptures taught that his sovereignty ensures that before the beginning of the world, God chose the elect to be "holy to himself" and had written their names in the book of life, "that all their salvation resteth wholly upon his hand and holy counsel that can by no means be altered or changed." Neither death, the devil, nor hell "dare now accuse them that are by adoption grafted in Christ, who are called of the eternal purpose...." Justification is put into the hearts of the elect by the Holy Spirit, and the glad tidings of the assurance of redemption provoke faith in the elect but condemnation in the reprobate, in order that human pride might be beaten down before the glory and honor of God.[32]

So that resisting the power of God he perisheth in this world, and in the world to come he is appointed to the everlasting fire prepared for the devil and his angels by the just judgment of the Almighty Lord: who being refused and so openly resisted, justly doth give over the wicked to their own reprobate minds.... This Reprobation then is the declaration of God his severe justice and just judgment, against the serpent and his seed, whom, by the word of his eternal wisdom he hath accursed from the beginning and appointed to everlasting torment.[33]

As with Beza, Gilby was anxious to preserve God from the authorship of sin; the scriptures clearly teach that sin is of the reprobates' own doing, for the sovereignty of God demands that he be free to make of his vessels whatever he chooses. That all people are shut under sin allowed God to show mercy. The good works which proceed from the Spirit of adoption, and the feeling of God's mercies within the elect, declare the glory of God and the presence of the spirit of Christ in order that they might be conformed to his eternal image. Good works, in this context, are a necessary consequence of predestination. We have been saved by the grace of an all-powerful and all-merciful God when we were lost in sin. This is a mystery which can only be understood in faith, and only God can grant the knowledge from above with which we can approach such mystery.[34]

Gilby's initial publication on the doctrine of predestination had been in 1553 and was a commentary on Malachi. Its focus was the statement, "Jacob I loved, Esau I hated," and it stirred the Englishman to offer his own commentary on God's election of some but his condemnation of others. That work is no longer extant, in fact, Gilby intimates that much of it perished, but would that alone inspire him to write another treatise on the subject when he had just finished reading Beza's treatment? Should we agree with Hargrave that Gilby's 1556 treatise was intended as a companion or supplement to Beza's treatise to which he appended some "additional lines for the unlearned"?[35] John Stockwood must have thought so, for he placed the two works together between the same covers, together with a tract on predestination by John Foxe, in *The Treasure of Truth* in 1576 and again in 1581.[36]

It is clear that there are marks of similarity between the treatises of Beza and Gilby. Both argue from the starting-point of God's sovereignty, both are supralapsarian, both wrote of the double decree, both were concerned to keep God from the authorship of sin, both saw the necessity of good works as corollary to predestination, and both end their treatises by highlighting the mystery of the doctrine. Two points, however, should be clarified. First, Gilby had already taken the matter of the double decree and the rejection of the reprobate further than what can be discerned in the marginalia of the 1560 Geneva Bible. In the latter, the severity of God's treatment of the reprobate is clearly not as aggressive or dominant as in either Beza's or Gilby's treatises. Still there is no question that double predestination is evident in the prefaces and annotations of Romans in the Geneva Bible.[37] It might even be conjectured that Gilby was the mind and hand behind the Romans marginalia in the Geneva Bible. Second, because Gilby's thought antedates Beza's treatise, it is difficult to postulate which one of the reformers influenced the other. Calvin's double decree does not appear until the 1559 *Institutes*, although he could easily have shared similar ideas with Beza and others prior to their publication.[38]

The point is that Gilby's double decree position is earlier than Beza's or Calvin's, and yet the similarity between Gilby and Beza is greater than his affinity with Calvin. Perhaps it was left to Beza to write a more sophisticated (scholastic?) work while Gilby initiated discussion of the doctrine with his more biblical orientation as represented in his earlier commentary of 1553.

But the exiles' predestinarian theology does not seem to represent the view of a limited atonement, although they seem scarcely far from doing so. Gilby still could write that Christ died for all to indicate God's universal grace, but how this coincides with his congruity with Beza's supralapsarianism and limited atonement is not worked out explicitly or in detail. The exiles saw no necessity to decipher dilemmas that their doctrine of God and his omnipotent and omniscient sovereignty created. What God's sovereignty implies for human freedom was not an issue for them; the important considerations were human responsibility for sin and God's merciful choosing of the elect. Because of human frailty and finitude, ours is not to probe the mysteries of divine providence.[39]

The importance given the doctrine of predestination can be gauged by how salvation is understood as intrinsic to God's sovereign plan. Because of the hardening of the hearts of the reprobate, the mercy of God does not apply to them; his mercy only pertains to those in whose hearts the Spirit moves to quicken for salvation. Salvation is by grace alone; the elect are saved by God's free act of mercy. The human being is helpless until God calls him by his Spirit. Thus faith itself is a gift of God, and no work of merit or good-will has any effect in redemption from sin. Righteousness is imputed upon the elect as God accepts us inspite of our imperfections and frailty. The law serves to remind us of our human condition before God and how we are helpless without divine succor.

During his exile, Thomas Sampson became adamant in his understanding of the Protestant doctrine of justification, a doctrine he was convinced the papists undermined with their many distinctions between "first" and "second" grace, "grace president" and "grace concomitating," "merit of congruence" and "merit of condignity" and a host of other conundrum. His own view was clear:

> That by nature ye are the children of wrath of yourselves: as of yourselves that ye are but such a lump of sin, that in you dwelleth no good thing. For which the law justly condemneth you as guilty of Gods curse and wrath, and so driveth you to Christ. By whose grace ye be freely justified. By whose bloodsheding, only and alone, the atonement is now made between God and you, which you believing are made the heirs of blessing of which your consciences by faith being assured by the work of Gods spirit, ye be at peace

with God because ye do feel even in your hearts by lively persuasion of faith
that Christ hath loved you, and given himself for you. For whose only sake
ye are justified and saved: which you thus feeling are led by the same spirit
that worketh this in you to render unto God the sacrifice of your body in
living and doing those works which in his sight are acceptable....[40]

Sampson believed that good works count for nothing with God,
for after all we can do we are still unprofitable servants. But through
faith in Christ human works are made pure and the good we do is done
by the Spirit of God working within us so that the "perfection of Gods
regenerate child" is the result.

One finds a similar emphasis in Beza's tract translated by
Whittingham in 1556. The law causes the recollection and recognition of sin, in turn producing fear in the heart. But the law's true purpose is to show humankind "that they should flee unto that only
mediator Jesus Christ." The severe and sharp preaching of God's law
thus is followed by the "grace and gentleness of the Gospel" so that
we might believe in Christ who alone can deliver from condemnation
and give us the power to obtain the heavenly inheritance. The
preaching of the word of God is accompanied by the inward manifes-
tation of the Holy Spirit who creates faith in the hearts of the elect,
bringing them to the knowledge of their election, "so that they begin
to will and to do the things which are of God."[41]

This tendency to view good works as concomitant to salvation is
reminiscent of William Tyndale as he began to work on his translation of the Pentateuch in the 1530s. His humanistic search for excel-
lence in moral philosophy began to take precedence over his distinc-
tively Lutheran emphasis of the mid-1520s. Luther's Law/Gospel
idea, coupled with the notion of *simul justus et peccator,* was set aside
by Tyndale to focus on "the moral code demanded by a stern God
whose pleasure was evoked by man's efforts to live out divine prescriptions for goodness."[42] Good works were not meritorious for faith
but remained prerequisite for righteousness just as a gift is prerequisite
to gratitude. It was the gratitude which changed for Tyndale, not the
gift. What fast became of first order for Tyndale as he began work on
Deuteronomic material within the Old Testament was the necessity of
law in order to show the validity and reliability of faith.

That the exiles were indebted to this Tyndalian idea rather than
what they imbibed from Calvin while sojourning in Geneva can be discerned by an examination of Calvin's teaching. Contrary to Tyndale,
Calvin taught that sanctification is not the purpose of justification for
both remain independent and Christ justifies no one whom he does not
sanctify at the same time. Sanctification will never become a perfect

reality in the Christian whereas justification is perfect from its inception. Thus we continue to be sinners even while we are being progressively sanctified and consequently there is a continual need for penitence. But Calvin could not resist the temptation, any more than Martin Bucer, to develop from his notion of sanctification a complete practical morality. Thus the Christian can derive from the scriptures a rule of conduct for daily life and advancement on the path toward holiness.[43]

Archbishop Cranmer reflected the Tyndalian emphasis in many of his homilies. That we are justified by grace alone through faith alone does not mean "that nothing should be required on our parts afterward." A faith which does not bring forth good works is not a "right, pure, and lively faith, but a dead, devilish, counterfeit, and feigned faith."[44]

The Geneva exiles taught a doctrine of salvation closely akin to Calvin which was characteristic of a pan-European movement of Protestant humanism led by Zwingli, Oecolampadius, Bucer, Capito, and Vadian. But this Protestant humanism had deep English roots in the thought of John Frith, Richard Taverner and William Tyndale, reformist preachers who continuously modified Lutheran doctrine "by the typical means of addition, emphasis, playing-down, and elimination of selected aspects which took account of changes occurring in the general milieu and thus enabled it to fit the English situation during the early Reformation."[45] The exiles' hinting of a limited atonement, their emphasis on sanctification as a sign of justification, and the covenantal understanding of law were quite different from what they would have imbibed on the Continent, especially in Geneva from Calvin's lectures and sermons. Indeed, it is safe to argue that there was an English Protestant tradition already in place from whose wisdom they could draw which defined their distinctive brand of puritan theology.

The distinctive English emphasis on ecclesiastical discipline and the addition of discipline and excommunication as the third mark of the true, visible church certainly can be better understood when placed in this context. Although ecclesiastical discipline is treated in the Geneva Bible marginalia, it is nowhere elevated as one of the marks of the visible church as it was in the *Forme of Prayers*, written by the exiles as their church order to direct the refugee church in Geneva. Calvin certainly saw the need for ecclesiastical discipline, but he was convinced, along with Beza, that the only two marks were preaching the word and correct administration of the sacraments. When the exiles exulted in the "pure discipline" of Geneva, they were reminisc-

ing more their own English ecclesiology than they were that indigenous to Geneva.[46]

III. THE CHURCH: WORSHIP, LITURGY
AND POLITY

While the English exiles were in Geneva, they published two important documents which exemplify their ecclesiology. In 1556, *The
forme of prayers and Ministration of the Sacraments* appeared as a
guide to the life of the church; three years later the *Boke of Psalms*
appeared as a kind of appendix.

It will be remembered that during the "Troubles at Frankfurt"
Whittingham and Knox had sent to Calvin a Latin synopsis of the
Edwardian Prayerbook which they had written, and which some historians are convinced was biased. In the meantime, the radical group
headed by Whittingham at Frankfurt attempted to assimilate a new
church order in January 1555; it was to have been the work of a
committee composed of Knox, Whittingham, Gilby, Foxe and
William Cole. It was not well received by the church and was never
used in Frankfurt. Yet it was this church order which became the substance of the *Forme of Prayers* which was used in the Geneva refugee
church. It was primarily Whittingham's genius which lay behind the
document. The confession of faith also contained a preface, a collection of fifty metered psalms, and Calvin's catechism translated into
English, and bore the epithet, "approved by the famous and godly
learned man, John Calvin." A Latin translation, *Ratio et Forme*, was
submitted to Calvin.[47]

The preface, "To Our Brethren in England, and elsewhere which
love Jesus Christ unfainedly, mercie, and peace," is in the same family
with the sentiment reflected in the prefaces of the 1560 Geneva Bible,
even to the degree of identical wording. The same Deuteronomic view
of history pervades every paragraph of the 1556 confession of faith.
God had shown great mercies upon England, but now the nation had
fallen into judgment because of unfaithfulness and idolatry; what was
needed was repentance for "now the day of visitation is come, and the
Lord hath brought the plagues upon us, whereof before we were ad-
monished, and most justly menaced." False prophets have deceived
with lies and the word of God is scarcely preached or practiced.[48]

Moreover, the preface indicates that the exiles believed that the
English congregations in exile should become examples of sound doctrine and apostolic church polity to the motherland. They were especially convinced that the accompanying order was done strictly ac-

cording to the limits of God's word and that no superfluous ceremony had been added to what could be prescribed by Holy Writ. "Ceremonies" have always been a problem for the church, even from apostolic times with foot washing and the supper after communion. Psalm-singing had biblical support and precedence, and putting psalms into meter was a worthwhile venture if those "skillful in the Hebrew tongue" who "easily may perceive the metre" were allowed to exercise their talents. It was important to maintain the "Hebrew sense" in such metered psalms. And, they were very pleased to include Calvin's catechism since they could find none better.[49]

The *Forme of Prayers* followed the Apostles' Creed, with the text and commentary replete with scriptural citations. Most of the confession is fairly straightforward and reflects the Reformed tradition consistently, and there would have been little with which Calvin could not agree, with the possible exception of the article on the church with its emphasis on the three marks of the true, visible church. The exiles were obviously concerned with the nature of Christ's person vis à vis the doctrine of transubstantiation. The corporal presence of Christ is in heaven at the right hand of God but nevertheless also present with the elect in spirit, power and grace. The church was not visible to human eyesight, "but only known to God, who of the lost sons of Adam hath ordained some as vessels of wrath, to damnation, and hath chosen others, as vessels of his mercy, to be saved." In order that we might seek and find God's elect, God provides three signs: "the word of God contained in the old and new testament...so it is left for all degrees of men, to read and understand"; the sacraments, not to be worshipped in any way, of baptism and the Lord's Supper, the former to bring us into God's family without imputation of sin, the latter to sustain us with the spiritual nourishment of our souls and the benefits of Christ's sacrificial death; and, ecclesiastical discipline "which standeth in admonition and correction of faults." The third mark, distinctive to English Reformers and not included in the Calvinist corpus of church orders,[50] had as its final end excommunication.

The confession contended that the magistrate belongs to the order of ecclesiastical law. The civil ruler "administers justice to every man, defending the good and punishing the evil," and to whom obedience is to be sworn as long as the government commands nothing contrary to scripture. Indeed, the magistrate is to purge the land of all false doctrine, whether Catholic or Anabaptist, including the mass, *Limbus Patrum*, celibacy and the doctrine of free will. All false teaching of papists, Anabaptists, "and such rascals or antichrist" must be purged just as Moses, Hezekiah and Josiah cleansed Israel of all idolatry, superstition and false religion.[51]

The minister should be in charge of public and private teaching, and he must also administer the sacraments. His work was to be primarily a counseling ministry, not an authoritative one, albeit he was to pronounce sentences of excommunication. The minister is to be chosen by the whole congregation, during the process of which the congregation is to fast and pray for eight days. If the minister is thus acceptable to the congregation, he is presented at the Sunday morning service by the current minister who was to have prepared that day's sermon on the qualifications and duties of ministers.[52]

The articles concerning elders and deacons were very much in line with the Calvinist corpus of church orders. Elders were to look after the congregation, governing with ministers, consulting, admonishing, correcting and ordering all things pertinent to the congregation. They neither preached nor administered the sacraments. The office of deacon was mainly to gather and distribute money among the poor and to serve the sick. The same procedure was followed in selecting elders and deacons as was prescribed in the selection of ministers, and both clergy and laymen could be considered as candidates for elders and deacons.[53]

The weekly assembly of ministers (or consistory) was to take place every Thursday. The purpose of the meeting was to address the faults and complaints which had come to the attention of the ministers, including their own demeanor as well. A list of vices is included in the church order, with those vices to which ministers were particularly vulnerable highlighted. One finds similar listing in the English translation of the *Lawes and Statutes of Geneva.*

Once each week the congregation was to assemble to hear "some place of the scriptures openly expounded." Any person could speak during this meeting as he was moved in his heart. Should problems arise in such an open forum, ministers and elders were expected to mitigate and take charge.[54]

The *Forme of Prayers* contained confessions of sin. "A Confession of our Sins, framed to our time, out of the 9. chapt. of Daniel" appears to have been a general confession, with particular focus on the sins of idolatry which characterized erstwhile days in England. As usual, a clear Deuteronomic motif is discernible. Another confession "for all states and times" follows, a characteristically Reformed confession of human guilt and inactivity, and the relentless reliance on God's mercy as provided in the death of Christ. Good works are needed, not to create worth but to exemplify the merits of Christ. Then a psalm was sung "in a plain tune" and the minister offered a prayer of supplication before proceeding to the sermon.

A prayer "for the whole estate of Christ's church" followed. Among other considerations the congregation was to pray for magistrates, especially local officials of Geneva. They also should pray for "our miserable country England" which once knew the mercy of God but now stands in need of his pity because of her bondage to idolatry. Furthermore, the congregation was to pray that "ravenous wolves" be rooted out while those persecuted and imprisoned be spared. The minister then pronounced the blessings of Numbers 6.8 and 2 Corinthians 13.13 upon the whole congregation.

The order of baptism disallowed female administration. The sacrament was not to be held in "private corners" but demonstrable to the public.[55] Infant baptism was practiced, the father and godfather accompanying the child to the church. A sermon was preached, and after the presentation of the child by the father and godfather, another sermon was delivered which likened baptism to circumcision. Instructions were then given the child, the father (or godfather in his absence) rehearsed the articles of faith, the child was named and then baptized with water upon its head. The child was then presented to God.[56]

The order of the Lord's Supper stipulated participation once each month. The officiating minister was to read 1 Corinthians 11 emphasizing in his remarks the importance of self-examination while partaking of the sacrament. The purpose of the supper was not to bring the congregation together in order that they might "protest" their uprightness or orderliness, but in order to seek life and perfection in Christ while acknowledging their spiritual sickness and depravity. Thus the true eating of Christ's body and blood is the acknowledgment of imperfection and sin and the necessity of reliance upon the merits of Christ's death. There is no change within the bread and wine but souls are nourished by faith in the reception of Christ "above the worldly and sensible" level. The minister then blessed the bread and gave thanks whereupon the congregation received the elements in distribution among themselves. The minister closed with a prayer of dedication and the people sang Psalm 103. A brief note is appended for the reader to explain that no papistical emphasis had been allowed in the service, and that the proper, spiritual significance of the sacrament had been identified since a sacrament signifies, and Christ was bodily present at the right hand of God. Thus no transubstantiation takes place as if the priest were speaking magical words.[57]

The marriage service was to be proceeded by several days during which the congregation was to consider whether any person had claim or title to either of the candidates for marriage. At the actual ceremony the minister exhorted the couple with paraphrases of a number of New Testament passages, emphasizing the necessity of each man having a wife because of the temptation to fornication. He spoke analogously of the body of Christ being undefiled from fornication and adultery and the importance of keeping the vessel of the Holy Spirit unpolluted. Otherwise, the ceremony was fairly traditional, although there was no wedding ring.[58]

The *Forme and Prayers* also contained brief prescriptions for visitation of the sick and burial of the dead. As physician of the soul the minister takes the active role in both exigencies. In the burial service, the corpse was to be brought to the grave accompanied by the congregation, after which they departed to the church for a sermon on death and the resurrection.

The order of ecclesiastical discipline was given special treatment. "As no city, town, house, or family, can maintain their estate and prosper, without policy and governance" even so "the church of God, which requireth more purely to be governed than any city or family cannot without spiritual policy and ecclesiastical discipline continue, increase, and flourish."[59] Discipline is like the sinews of the body, knitting it together; it is like a bridle to stay the wicked from mischief, a spur to prick forward such as are slow and negligent. In short, it is God's way of keeping the church in good order. If it be asked why the church must have discipline, the first answer is that no people of "evil conversation" may be allowed to enter the church. Second, it is important for the good to continue in their goodness and not be contaminated by evil infection. Third, when excommunication is finally pronounced, the guilty will turn with shame from his fault and come to repentance in order that his soul might be saved.

The Bible recognizes the difference between private and public discipline; for example, when one is at fault, he may be approached individually, but should he persist, several witnesses should be called until ultimately his persistence brings him before the whole congregation, either to be acquitted and reinstated or excommunicated and punished. All must be done in love and must proceed with modesty and wisdom. When the matter becomes public it is the duty of ministers and elders to exercise their leadership, but the whole church must be made aware of the problem and participate in the disciplinary process. The excommunicant was not to be forbidden audience at sermons, however, for sermons may help him to repent. He was not allowed to receive the sacraments and was discharged from all other duties of the church.[60]

The *Forme of Prayers* then included "One and Fiftie Psalms of David in Englishe metre...," thirty-seven of which were taken from Sternhold and at least seven from Hopkins. The remaining metered psalms were anonymous but Whittingham and perhaps Kethe were the likely authors.[61] A brief note before each psalm indicates its content; these are almost verbatim with the notes which precede the psalms in the 1560 Geneva Bible.

Calvin's catechism followed. The catechism preceded the last item in the *Forme and Prayers*, a devotional itinerary of prayers and blessings which provided a "[f]orme of prayers to be vsed in privat houses euery morninge, and euenyngs." There were prescribed morning prayers, prayers to be said before meals, a thanksgiving after meals, evening prayers, and a prayer "made at the first assemble of the congregation, [w]hen the confession of our faithe, and [w]hole orders of the church [w]as there red, and approued."

In 1559 the *Boke of Psalmes* was published from Geneva by Rowland Hall. It was dedicated to Queen Elizabeth and appeared just shortly before the publication of the famous Geneva Bible of 1560. The "Arguments," annotations and text are identical in the *Boke of Psalms* and the Geneva Bible. The only difference between the former and the *Book of Psalms* in the latter was the prefaces and two tables which appear at both the beginning and end of the *Boke of Psalmes*. One table was an acrostic; the other a kind of topical break-down of the Psalms "containing the chief points of our belief comprehended in common places."[62]

What was unique about the *Boke of Psalmes* was its dedicatory preface to the Queen. In it the exiles vouchsafed that her fame would remain registered in the heavens if she sought after the heavenly wisdom of the "true Solomon" (likening Elizabeth to the Queen of Sheba who sought Solomon's wisdom) who is Christ. Christ had set England as an example of the "pattern of true religion and Christian life to imitate." The authors mentioned that they had begun more than a year before "to peruse the English translation of the sacred Bible" but until they could finish it they were desirous to see the *Boke of Psalmes* made public and to dedicate it to her majesty. There was hardly a part of the Bible more important, especially for those who rule. For example, David, the great monarch of Israel, had many problems befall him yet God never forsook him. Elizabeth must suppress papistry and let the word of God shine forth so that God "will bless you with godly posterity and maintain you in perfect peace and quietness." Again, this motif is the same that one finds in both the 1557 and 1560 editions of the Bible published by the Geneva exiles.

The exhortations to the reader include advise on how to use the Psalms; they should not be read repeatedly, but should be considered mirrors in which the infinite mercies of God toward his church during troubles and affliction are reflected. The authors also explained that when the Hebrew is difficult to translate, the words would be put in italics for the sake of clarity or some explanation would be appended in a footnote. The text of 1 Corinthians 13.4 closes the volume.

What seems clear about the exiles' view of the church and its new liturgy was its simplicity, order, intelligibility and fidelity to the scriptures. These characteristics had replaced the riches of tradition and the impressive mystery and pageantry of medieval worship which they had known in Henrican and Edwardian England. Now they were more participants than spectators, and ethics had replaced aesthetics. But above all, it was a restoration of the primitive practice of the apostolic church as they believed it to have been.

This restitutionist hermeneutic[63] was at the heart of Martin Bucer's *De Regno Christi*. But Bucer's restorationism was Constantinian insofar as the godly monarch was sovereign over a Christian theocracy, and while the exiles shared such a theocratic vision, what they wanted to restore antedated Constantine—the Golden Age of the apostles. The exiles were not really proto-separatists, for they still envisioned a national church built upon the solid foundation of a biblical, apostolic primitivism. The Calvinist notion of order and discipline which the exiles, unlike their Geneva mentor, made a third mark of the church implied strictly regulated church and civil governments. Their problem was that of refugees who increasingly became more radical by the experience of exile: how could their experience as a refugee congregational church be implemented within a national church context? What should prevent the sovereign from leading God's people according to the word of God, especially since England had a national covenant with God? The exiles' understanding of the church, therefore, coupled with their concern for order and discipline, if contextualized within a national framework, clearly led them to see England as God's new Israel, and to read the Bible as the blueprint of his ongoing activity in history both for and against them in accordance with their faithfulness to his law.[64]

IV. THE EUCHARIST

The common thread which ties together the various Reformed doctrines of the eucharist is the role of faith in the reception of the supper. Both Calvin and Bullinger believed that those who come to the supper without faith receive only the bare signs; what the faithful receive, in contrast, is the body and blood of Christ. Martin Bucer maintained that Christ was really present in the supper, *realiter et substantialiter*, on the condition that faith is the controlling factor.

Peter Martyr would have echoed the same sentiment: Christians receive the thing signified by faith. On the English side, this was also the view of Thomas Cranmer; even John Jewell declared that faith was necessary for the Christian to partake of the reality signified in the bread and the wine, although he characteristically seemed to place more stress on the activity of the believer.[65]

Consistent within this Reformed tradition, typified by the *Consensus Tigurinus*, was the activity of the Holy Spirit which effected the presence of the body and blood of Christ when the communicant partook of the signs by faith. Hence the objective element was accomplished by the Spirit in bringing about the reality of Christ's presence; the subjective element, also the work of the Spirit, produced faith in the heart of the believer. One finds varying shades of this motif in Calvin, Bullinger and Bucer, with Peter Martyr advocating more of a sacramental mutation, i.e. the elements are mutated from common to sacramental things, signifying the body and blood of Christ. The English Reformed eucharistic theology, represented by Cranmer, was very much in line with this tradition, although Jewell seemed reluctant to enunciate a clear doctrine of the Spirit in his eucharistic thought. It has been suggested that the reason Jewell seemed reluctant to delve into the Spirit's work was the polemical context of his writing and the necessity therefore to adumbrate the remotest position from the Roman doctrine of transubstantiation.[66]

There is merit in this suggestion. The polemical context of much of the eucharistic theology in England precipitated the rough edges of the discussion with the result that many English reformers tried to steer a course as far away from transubstantiation as possible. Thus John Frith, William Tyndale, John Hooper and Thomas Becon were essentially memorialists like Zwingli and Oecolampadius.[67] It was this memorialist tradition which characterizes much of the eucharistic thought of the Geneva exiles.

When Anthony Gilby answered the Roman Catholic Stephen Gardiner, a Henrican bishop, in 1547 he accused him of duplicating arguments from arid scholasticism. Gilby thought that the doctrine of the eucharist should be modeled on biblical grounds without imposition by extraneous argumentation from medieval schoolmen. Chief among matters to which Gilby objected was the doctrine of transubstantiation and the hermeneutical apparatus necessary to defend it. If one were forced to take literally every passage in the New Testament which Romanists used to bolster transubstantiation, the hermeneutical mess had only begun.

Gilby's approach was what he thought was more direct and common sensical. The bread and the wine remain bread and wine, but inwardly to the soul they are the body and blood of the Lord. Gilby constantly stressed the difference between a sign and what it signified and how the two cannot logically be identical. There is no mention of faith which brings to life the thing signified, nor is there any reference to the work of the Holy Spirit. The thrust of Gilby's polemic was the emphatic denial of the doctrine of transubstantiation and the perversion of sound principles of biblical interpretation which accompanied it.[68]

In 1554, Thomas Sampson wrote briefly concerning the eucharist from Strasburg before coming to Geneva two years later. The sacrament, to Sampson, was a "commemoration" of the body and blood of Christ which was to be partaken by faith. As with Gilby, Sampson's main preoccupation was the denial of transubstantiation and the problematic hermeneutical principles necessary to uphold such a doctrine. There was no sacrifice in the celebration of the mass, for the supper of the Lord was a sacrament which allowed the Christian to partake of the elements which by faith become Christ's real presence. Sampson's view is closer to the Reformed views of Bucer, Calvin and Cranmer ("virtualism") than Gilby's if for no other reason than the explicit inclusion of faith as a necessary component to ensure the real presence for the faithful. Still, Sampson does not introduce the work of the Holy Spirit into his discussion.[69]

We have seen that Whittingham wrote a preface to Nicholas Ridley's treatise on the Lord's Supper during his exile in 1556. Ridley's treatise has been labeled "the best-argued treatise on the Eucharist from the Protestant side in sixteenth century England."[70] Ridley had advised Cranmer, and along with Bucer's *Censura Martini Buceri super libro sacorum*, had played a definite role in influencing the eucharistic thought of the Archbishop of Canterbury. It was Ridley who confessed that the figurative interpretation of the elements in the Lord's Supper had been introduced to him by Ratramnus whose ninth-century treatise had been reprinted in Cologne in 1531 at Oecolampadius' instigation.[71] It is difficult to determine how much Ridley's thought paralleled that of Whittingham since the latter wrote nothing outside the Geneva Bible marginalia on the eucharist. Still, to have sanctioned Ridley's treatise with a preface should indicate some degree of positive endorsement.

Ridley's conclusions were much like those of Gilby and Sampson, perhaps because Ridley's treatise also focused on the denial of transubstantiation. He shared with Gilby the displeasure of scholastic sophistry as well as Gilby's use of Augustine and the church fathers. Ridley was desirous to show the sacramentarian presence of Christ in the elements. The bread and the wine remained the same, the bread at the altar, the wine in the chalice, but sacramentally they were the real body and blood of Christ to the faithful, "food of life and immortality." What Ridley meant by "sacrament" is not altogether clear, but he unequivocally acknowledged that he believed in more than a signification of the real presence in the elements. Ridley was convinced that there was a real presence of Christ within the elements of bread and wine, although the presence of Christ is spiritual and not physical.

The Geneva Bible marginalia contain a number of references to sacraments because sacraments were given the people of God to signify their salvation, although a sacrament becomes invalid when it is practiced without a sincere heart. Circumcision was called the covenant between God and Israel "& hath the promise of grace joined to it," a promise common to all sacraments. The ark of the covenant was a sacrament to Israel for it signified the presence of God to the nation. Thus "the sign is taken for the thing signified, which is common to all sacraments both in the old & new testament." The paschal lamb was thus not the passover "as sacraments are not the thing itself, which they do represent, but signify it."[72]

It appears that the exiles who contributed to the Geneva Bible favored a sacramentarian or memorialist doctrine of the eucharist. They constantly reminded the reader that a sacrament signifies or represents spiritual reality and was not part of the reality itself.

> The bread is a true sign, and an assured testimony that the body of Jesus Christ is given for the nurture of our soules: likewise the wine signifieth that his blood is our drink to refresh and quicken us everlastingly.[73]

Although there is no explicit reference to transubstantiation in the annotations, doubtless the translators felt they were undermining such a doctrine with their emphasis on the representative nature of sacraments. Perhaps there was some anti-transubstantiation polemic behind the comments on Jesus' affirmation that he was the "bread of life," for the translators wrote "it cometh of the power of the Spirit that the flesh of Christ giveth us life."[74]

The Geneva Bible marginalia resonate with Gilby's eucharistic thought more than any other point-of-view we have studied. There is the constant dialectic of the sign or sacrament (used interchangeably) and what the sign points to. When God gives a sign or a sacrament what it points to or what it fulfills is inherent within God's promise. The bread and wine were signs of Christ's body and blood and not only pointed to these realities but guaranteed a sacramental or spiritual presence of the Lord's body and blood to nurture and refresh the faithful. The marginalia stop short of explicitly mentioning the partaking of the elements by faith or the mysterious work of the Holy Spirit, although both are clearly implied.

Gilby and the Geneva Bible annotations therefore appear more Zwinglian or memorialist than Sampson or Whittingham's choice, Ridley, whose views are closer to Calvin, Bucer, Bullinger and Cranmer. This points out again the importance of the mind and hand of Anthony Gilby, for his theology never seems in tension with the theological sentiment flowing throughout the Geneva Bible marginalia. It is safe to argue, nonetheless, that the eucharistic theology of the Geneva exiles was not uniform or univocal; indeed, the exiles were attempting primarily to explicate a biblical model of the eucharist, bequeathed from Erasmus and a transnational Protestant humanism, which stood in stark contrast to the Roman doctrine of transubstantiation. They reveal little cognizance of their continuity or discontinuity with the Continental Reformed tradition and the different nuances of its eucharistic thought.

V. CHURCH AND STATE

Gottfried Locher has suggested that every flight into exile is a political criticism and "simultaneously contains indeed an anarchistic element."[75] This certainly was true for the Geneva exiles. Perhaps more than anything else it was the political ideology that emerged from Geneva which spelled doom for the careers of John Knox and Christopher Goodman in England. The rest of the exiles became guilty by association with the sentiments expressed in Goodman's *How Svperior Powers Oght to be Obeyd* and Knox's *First Blast of the Trumpet Against the Monstrovs Regiment of Women.*

Both Goodman and Knox advocated civil disobedience when matters reached a crucial stage in the administration of an ungodly tyrant. Goodman taught that inferior magistrates such as parliament had the first responsibility to diffuse the wrongdoing of an ungodly magistrate, but if this were unsuccessful in redressing the situation for the good of true religion, the common people have the right to resist. In short, Goodman's political theory was that parliament should depose Mary and be willing to shed her blood to wrest from her the throne. If parliament failed to meet its responsibility and the cause of true religion continued to be jeopardized, the populace had the right to disobey civil law and engage in a violent overthrow of the ungodly tyrant. The rationale for tyrannicide was the biblical mandate that Christians are to obey God rather than man. If Godly people could not entertain exile, they should resist as the final duty of the warrior of God.[76]

John Knox had come to a similar conclusion, as did John Ponet while exiled in Strasburg.[77] Knox had been wrestling with the issue of civil disobedience for some time before the *First Blast* appeared in 1558. It is known that Pierre Viret was a frequent visitor to Geneva between 1553 and 1559, and he could have influenced Knox and Goodman with his radical political ideas.[78] It is not possible, nor is it necessary, to trace Goodman's and Knox's political theology to Continental origins, however. It is not known whether Knox influenced Goodman or vice-versa, or whether each came to his political ideas independent of the other. It would certainly seem likely that two ministers of the same refugee congregation would confer on such important issues. Still, Knox was in and out of Geneva frequently, and Goodman and Anthony Gilby probably had at least as much discussion about church and state matters as did the Scot with either of them.

Knox's treatise continued Goodman's polemic against gynecocracy, but the Scot went beyond Goodman's biblical rationale by appealing to nature, history, civil law, the church fathers, and even Aristotle. The strongest argument against female sovereignty came from the Bible, however, and the lessons that the nation of Israel learned should serve as a mandate for England. Like Goodman, Knox looked to inferior magistrates to redress wrongdoing, but when that failed the common people had the right to resist. When the nobility or parliament failed to resist Mary Tudor, thereby failing to emulate Israel's resistance of Jezabel and the usurper Queen Athaliah, the path to civil, violent resistance was the only one left to uphold true religion. Bowler says it well:

> This was truly radical stuff and, had it ever been adopted, would have swept away English constitutional law and custom, the rule of women, dynastic monarchy and the possibility of anyone but an enthusiastic Calvinist male sitting on the throne.[79]

Anthony Gilby also had stern warnings for the people of England and Scotland, and he was not afraid to append his name to Knox's controversial writings of 1558 in the form of prefaces to both *A Faithful Admonition* and *The Appellation* in which Knox's full-blown tyrannicidal and anti-gynecocratic prejudices first became apparent. In his own writings, Gilby stopped short of the radical positions of Goodman and Knox, for he never openly advocated tyrannicide, although he approximated his fellow exiles' judgment regarding female rule in *An Admonition to England and Scotland*. He made no distinction that inferior magistrates had the primary duty to resist an ungodly tyrant.

The Geneva Bible marginalia have been the target of not a few accusations of prejudicial and reactionary views of civil government, yet one can find both continuity and discontinuity with the Goodman-Knox ideology in the annotations. Throughout, the Deuteronomic view of retribution prevails since the wickedness of the king brings God's wrath upon the "whole realm." God has given special duties to the magistrate and he is directly answerable to God for bringing peace and religious tranquillity to the commonwealth. It is impossible to govern well without "continual study of Gods word," and where there is no magistrate who fears God "there can be no true religion...nor order." If rulers are obstinate and become tyrants, "it is a sign that God hath drawn back his countenance and favor from that place." In the reign of a good magistrate like David there will always be "most great plenty, both of fruit & also of the increase of mankind."[80]

There is a definite "anti-tyrant" motif which runs throughout the annotations. There are constant references to wicked craftiness, "open rage," and oppression of "true religion." Instructions for magistrates are commonplace. During Israel's economy, the civil magistrate was required to consult the high priest prior to a decision, thus indicating that the civil lord "could execute nothing but that which he knew to be the will of God." Hezekiah became the paragon of all sovereigns because he established pure religion. Such a good monarch "ought to be so dear unto his people...that they will rather lose their lives, than that ought should come unto him." The glory and wealth of a nation "standeth in their preservation of the godly magistrate." It is the duty of subjects to honor and reverence the office of the king and to obey his every precept as long as it does not conflict with God's law.[81] Christians are to honor magistrates, even should they be infidels, as long as they "command us nothing against the word of God." But when Jeremiah 29.7 recorded that we should pray for the magistrate, the compilers noted:

> The prophet speaketh not this for the affection that he bore to the tyrant, but that they should pray for the commonrest, and quietness, that their troubles might not be increased, and that they might with more patience and less grief wait for the time of their deliverance.[82]

A clear distinction should be made between the tone of the annotations on the Old Testament with those on the New Testament. The New Testament annotations are less judgmental and reactionary whereas the annotations on Old Testament passages are preoccupied with the wickedness and idolatry which characterized many civil administrations in the history of Israel. The annotations in Ezekiel, for example, compare tyrants to "cruel and huge beasts which devour all that be weaker than they, and such as they may overcome." The New Testament annotations avow that kings and princes had their rightful and God-given roles, and many of them will have their names inscribed in the "Book of Life." The comment on Revelation 21.24 reads,

> [H]ere we see as in infinite other places that Kings & Princes (contrary to that wicked opinion of the Anabaptists) are partakers of the heavenly glory, if they rule in the fear of the Lord.[83]

The Geneva Bible marginalia do not support the tyrannicidal and anti-gynecocratic views of Goodman and Knox, and there are places in the annotations where Anabaptist views of the state were condemned. The New Testament gave the compilers grounds for supporting the divine right of magistrates, and although the notes on Old Testament passages are clearly more stern and judgmental of tyrants, the Deuteronomic theory of retribution allowed the compilers to attribute harsh and fatal treatment of tyrants to God's just judgment. As with the political theology of Anthony Gilby, the annotations give no mandate to inferior magistrates the primary right of resistance. Indeed, Gilby's stance seems more like the Old Testament notes whereas the New Testament notes would have been more commensurate with Calvin and the political theology of Geneva.

Whittingham had written the preface to Goodman's controversial book after hearing him preach his sermon on the text in Acts, "We Must Obey God rather than Men." The question, of course, is why: did Whittingham endorse Goodman's (and therefore Knox's) tyrannicidal and anti-gynecocratic ideology? It would be risky to affirm such. Most of the annotations of Whittingham's 1557 New Testament were carried over into the 1560 marginalia which, as we have suggested, are considerably softer in tone than marginalia in the Old Testament. Of all the exiles, Whittingham may have been the most sensitive to Calvin's ideas; that Calvin would become embarrassed and miffed, indeed angered, by the sentiments of Goodman and Knox in their writings likely weighed heavily on Whittingham's heart.

What remains of the exiles' view of church and state is that Goodman and Knox adumbrated a political theology of the most radical sort, and no Continental figure had arrived at a similar conviction. Moreover, neither Goodman nor Knox got his ideas from Calvin or Beza.[84] Once again, the influence of Calvin upon the English

Protestant exiles was minimal; it appears that they had their own tradition, even their own agenda.

VI. A NATION IN COVENANT WITH GOD

Richard Bauckham is convinced that the seeds of England as an elect nation were "sown by the defeat of the Armada, not before."[85] The writings of the Geneva exiles which we have examined written before, during and after their exile on the Continent, however, present clear counter-evidence to Bauckham's claim. The idea of England as a nation in covenant with God pervades almost everything these early puritans wrote. This Deuteronomic view of history along with its corollary of divine retribution can be traced back at least as early as William Tyndale's commentaries on the Pentateuch and Jonah. The exiles looked back to England upon a motherland whose rejections of the Protestant progressions tendered under Edward VI and his supporters had resulted in plague and pestilence. When Elizabeth ascended to the throne, the exiles praised her Protestant upbringing and preparation and likened her to reformer monarchs in Israel's economy. Were she to lead faithfully in accordance with her Protestant billing, heavenly succor and success were guaranteed; were she to devolve toward Catholicism God's judgment would stand fast against the nation.[86]

Tyndale's shift from Lutheranism to a covenant theology has not escaped the notice of historians. Both L. J. Trinterud and J. G. Møller have focused on how Tyndale abandoned Wittenberg for Zurich and followed Zwingli's idea of a covenant as Zwingli struggled with his defense of paedobaptism against the Anabaptists. To Zurich, the covenant between God and humankind was an agreement between two parties, the consequence of which was that man must fulfill certain conditions in order to receive the blessings of the divine promise. This was somewhat different from Calvin's emphasis. For Calvin, the covenant is not so much an agreement as God's eternal promise to humankind which culminates in Jesus Christ. There are conditions, of course, but these are endemic to the dynamic nature of the covenant as initiated by God who predestined the elect in his mercy.[87] What the exiles did was to combine these two emphases: from Zwingli and the Zurich tradition through Oecolampadius and Bullinger, the notion of conditional, contractual obligation; from Calvin and the Geneva tradition, the preeminence of salvation by grace as exercised by God within a predestinarianism. But the combining contributed by the exiles had the additional federalist component of England as God's new Israel.

English Protestants, including the Genevan exiles, superimposed what they learned from Calvin, particularly the doctrine of predestination, upon a theology they already had, which included the idea of a national covenant following the Deuteronomic view of history.[88]

This "Israelite paradigm" was a move from individual to society by way of a monistic shift away from a platonic dualism which separates the individual from society. The result was the individual and the society become almost indistinguishable so that the individual is the society in microcosm and the society the individual in macrocosm. Thus Calvin's covenant of grace became intertwined with a national or federal ethos calling for amendment of life, repentance and reconciliation. As such, it was not strictly a covenant of works, and at that point abandoned its Zurich emphasis for the characteristically English puritan emphasis.[89] What the Zurichian "covenant of works" had provided these early puritans was a way of "bringing the unregenerate majority...clearly within the covenantal design through a legal bond with the Deity."[90]

Christopher Goodman's *How Svperior Powers Oght to be Obeyd* is filled with the motif of England as God's chosen nation. Anthony Gilby's commentaries as well as his *Admonition to England and Scotland* offer a clear example of a reformer who views himself as a prophet of God calling his elect people back to the old paths of biblical religion. No clearer evidence needs to be marshaled than the Geneva Bible marginalia, and in particular the "Preface to the Queen." Reading the history of Israel as the prototype of their own nation elected by the Deity who reveals itself in history, the Geneva exiles sought to show that rewards and punishments were given by divine mandate according to the faithfulness to the covenant that God had made with his people. England was God's new Israel, in covenant bond with him, for the purpose of realizing his kingdom among the people of the nation of England.[91]

Thus the thrust of the exiles' covenant theology was England's status as an elect nation under God, and that the commonwealth's faithfulness to God's covenant with his new Israel was the measure of current events. They could expect blessing and honor for faithfulness but curse and rejection for idolatry. The exiles' combining of Zurichian and Genevan covenant ideas with an underpinning of federalism characterizes no other Protestant tradition of the sixteenth century. As Patrick Collinson suggests, these puritan voices were willing to follow Calvin's theocentrism as long as they could couch it within the well-being of the people of God, and it was this which Martin Bucer contributed during Edward VI's reign in *De Regno Christi*: a social doctrine of the church which helped "to lay ecclesiological foundations for a Protestant politics and social policy by his own thorough socialization in the civic life."[92] That is a subject which deserves further attention.

This federalist emphasis which pervades the covenant theology of the Geneva exiles was endemic to the English Reformation. Hugh Latimer could refer to "Our Lord God, God of England, for verily he hath shewed Himself God of England, or rather an English God." Archbishop Parker would echo the same sentiment, "...where almighty God is so much English as he is," and Catherine Parr would look back to Henry VIII and liken him to Moses leading England out of the bondage of Romanism and the new king, Edward VI, as a second Josiah or another Constantine. This was at the heart of the Tudor puritan covenant theology; in the words of John Hooper, it meant to "purge this Church of England to the purity and sincerity of God's word."[93]

NOTES

[1] See John S. Coolidge, *The Pauline Renaissance in England. Puritanism and the Bible* (London: Clarendon Press, 1970), pp. 141–50.

[2] Horton Davies, *Worship and Theology in England from Cranmer to Hooker, 1534–1603* (Princeton: Princeton University Press, 1970), p. 15.

[3] *The Geneva Bible: A Facsimile of the 1560 Edition*, ed. L. E. Berry (Madison: University of Wisconsin Press, 1969), Preface to the Queen, fo. iii, r.

[4] *Ibid.*, annotations on Ps. 119.45, fo. 281, r; Jer. 19.5, fo. 312, v; Mic. 4.2, fo. 375, r; Matt. 16.19, fo. 19, r; I Cor. 15.3, fo. 81, v.

[5] *Ibid.*, annotation on Matt. 5, fo. 3, v.

[6] From Whitgift, *Works* (Parker Soc.), I, 17, quoted in Porter, *Puritanism in Tudor England*, p. 2.

[7] Porter, pp. 3–6.

[8] *Ibid.*, p. 8. See also Philip Edgcumbe Hughes, *Theology of the English Reformers* (London: Hodder and Stoughton, 1965), pp. 38–39.

[9] For a fuller discussion of primitivism or restitutionism, see James C. Spalding, "Restitution as a Normative Factor for Puritan Dissent," *Journal of the American Academy of Religion*, 44 (1976), 47–63.

[10] *An Admonition to Parliament,* fo. Ai, v.

[11] *Ibid.*, fos. Biii, v–Bv, r. Cf. Gilby's translation of *The Psalms of David* by Beza, fo. A3, v.

[12] Fos. Av, v–Avi, r.

[13] Cambridge University Library, Baker Mss., Vol. 32, Mm. 1.43, pp. 427–30.

[14] See Strype, *Parker*, I, 322–33.

[15] Bernard J. Verkamp, *The Indifferent Mean: Adiaphorism in the English Reformation to 1554* (Athens: Ohio University Press, 1977), p. 162.

[16] *Ibid.*, pp. 163–72.

[17] *Ibid.*, p. 149. See also Bernard J. Verkamp, "The Zwinglians and Adiaphorism," *Church History* 42 (1973), 486–504.

[18] See Walter Philips, "Henry Bullinger and the Elizabethan Vestiarian Controversy: An Analysis of Influence," *Journal of Religious History* 11 (1981), 363–84. For the broader spectrum of Zurich's influence on the English Reformation, cf. Gottfried W. Locher, "Zwinglis Einflus in England und Schottland—Daten und Probleme," *Zwingliana* 14 (1975), 165–209.

[19] *Ibid.* See also J. H. Primus, *The Vestments Controversy: An Historical Study of the Earliest Tensions Within the Church of England in the Reign of Edward VI and Elizabeth* (N. V. Hampton, 1960), for a detailed discussion of the vestiarian controversy.

[20] Greaves, *Theology and Revolution in the Scottish Reformation: Studies in the Thought of John Knox*, pp. 26–29.

[21] R. T. Kendall, *Calvin and English Calvinism to 1649* (New York: Oxford University Press, 1979), p. 210.

[22] See John S. Bray, *Theodore Beza's Doctrine of Predestination* (Nieuwkoop: B. DeGraaf, 1975), pp. 137–43, *passim*; O. T. Hargrave, "The Predestinarian Offensive of the Marian Exiles at Geneva," *Historical Magazine of the Protestant Episcopal Church* 42 (1973), 111–23; and, Dewey D. Wallace, "The Doctrine of Predestination in the Early English Reformation," *Church History* 43 (1974), 201–15.

[23] Hargrave, "The Predestinarian Offensive...." Cf. François Wendel, *Calvin: The Origin and Development of His Religious Thought,* ts. Philip Mairet (London: Wm. Collins, 1963), pp. 263–77.

[24] Kendall, p. 210.

[25] Bray, pp. 137ff.

[26] *A Briefe declaration of the chiefe poyntes of Christian Religion, set forth in a Table* (Geneva: Printed by Jo. Rivery, 1556), found also in *The Treasure of Truth, touching the grounde work of man his salvation, and chiefest pointes of Christian Religion...and newly turned into English,* by Iohn Stockwood (London, 1581), fo. D1, v. See also Peter White, *Predestination, Policy and Polemic. Conflict and Consensus in the English Church from the Reformation to the Civil War* (Cambridge: University Press, 1992), pp. 16ff.

[27] *A Brief declaration*, fos. F4, v–F6, r.

[28] White, p. 20; Bray, pp. 104–05.

[29] *A Brief declaration*, fo. H4, v.

[30] *Ibid.*, fos. K6, v–K9, r.

[31] Hargrave, "The Predestinarian Offensive...."

[32] Anthony Gilby, *A Briefe Treatise on Election and Reprobation, with certen answers to the obiections of the aduersaries of thys doctrine* (Geneva, 1556), fos. Aii, v–Bii, v.

[33] *Ibid.,* fo. Biii, r.

[34] *Ibid.*, fos. Bvii, v–Ci, v.

[35] Hargrave, "The Predestinarian Offensive...."

[36] *Ibid.*

[37] See Dan G. Danner, "The Contribution of the Geneva Bible of 1560 to the English Protestant Tradition," *Sixteenth Century Journal* 12 (1981), 5–18; cf. Maurice S. Betteridge, "The Bitter Notes: The Geneva Bible and Its Annotations," *Sixteenth Century Journal* 14 (1983), 41–62.

[38] Cf., e.g., *A Commentarye upon the Epistle of Saint Paul to the Romans, written in Latine by M. Iohn Caluin, and newly translated into Englishe by Christopher Rosdell* (London: 1583), which illustrates the influence of Calvin's predestinarian ideas in their more developed form on English readers.

[39] See Ronald J. VanderMolen, "Providence as Mystery, Providence as Revelation: Puritan and Anglican Modifications of John Calvin's Doctrine of Providence."

[40] Thomas Sampson, *A letter to the trew professors of Christs Gospel...,* fo. Avi, r–v.

[41] *A Briefe declaration of the chief poyntes of Christian Religion...,* fos. F4, v–F6, r.

[42] William A. Clebsch, *England's Earliest Protestants 1520–1535* (New Haven: Yale University Press, 1964), p. 154.

[43] See *Institutes of the Christian Religion,* ts. and annot. by Ford Lewis Battles (Grand Rapids: Eerdmans, 1975), III.16.1; III.11.6; III.6.1.

[44] Thomas Cranmer, *Homily of Salvation* in *Miscellaneous Writings and Letters of Thomas Cranmer,* ed. for the Parker Society by John Edmund Cox (Cambridge: University Press, 1846), pp. 131–33.

[45] John K. Yost, "A Reappraisal of How Protestantism Spread during the Early English Reformation," *Anglican Theological Journal* 60 (1978), 437–46. Cf. Richard L. Greaves, "The Origins and Early Development of English Covenant Thought," *The Historian* 31 (1968), 21–35.

[46] Cf. Philippe Denis, "'Discipline' in the English Huguenot Churches of the Reformation: A Legacy or a Novelty?" *Proceedings of the Huguenot Society of London* 23 (1979), 166–71; James C. Spalding, "The *Reformatio Legum Ecclesiasticarum* of 1552 and the Furthering of Discipline in England," *Church History* 39 (1970), 162–71.

[47] See Maxwell, *John Knox's Genevan Service Book, 1556,* pp. 12ff. Maxwell has successfully shown that the *Ratio et Forma* was not derived from Poullain's *Liturgica sacra* but is a bona fide translation of the *Forme of Prayers.* See Maxwell, p. 5.

[48] *The forme of prayers and Ministration of the Sacraments, &c, vsed in the Englishe Congregation at Geneua: and approued, by the famous and godly learned man, Iohn Caluyn* (Imprinted at Geneva by Iohn Crespin, 1556), fol. Aii, v–Aiii, r.

[49] *Ibid.,* fo. Biii, v–Biv, v.

[50] Ecclesiastical discipline had been a concern of the radical Frankfurt group. They shared this distinction with Peter Martyr, but the tradition of discipline as the third mark goes back to Erasmus Sarcerius and his *Common places of scripture orderly...set forth...to the great profyte and help of all such studentes in gods worde...,* which had been translated into English by Richard Taverner in 1538. Whittingham had been a close associate of Martyr at Oxford and London. See Joseph C. McLelland, *The Visible Words of God* (Grand Rapids: Wm. B. Eerdmans, 1957), pp. 125ff.

[51] *Forme and Prayers,* fo. Ciii, v–Civ, v.

[52] *Ibid.,* fo. Cv, v–Cvii, v. Cf. Maxwell, pp. 58–60, and note the slight differences of how this practice differed from Calvin's and Pullain's church orders.

[53]*Forme and Prayers*, fo. Cvii, v. Interestingly, in smaller print, the authors indicated that they were quite aware of the office of teacher or doctor, but their condition in exile did not lend itself to the implementation of this office. In the future they would implement the office with schools and colleges where God's word could be taught and biblical languages mastered. See fo. Cviii, r–v.

[54]*Ibid.*, fo. Di, v–Dii, r.

[55]Recall that John Knox was adamant in his opposition to private baptisms. See Maxwell, p. 112.

[56]*Forme and Prayers*, fo. Dviii, r–Eiii, v.

[57]*Ibid.*, fo. Eiv, r–Eviii, r. Maxwell has an extensive discussion of the order of the Lord's Supper, pp. 121–43.

[58]*Forme and Prayers,* fo. Fii, r.

[59]*Ibid.*, fo. Fv, r.

[60]*Ibid.*, fo. Fv, r–Fvii, r. Cf. Denis, "'Discipline' in the English Huguenot Churches of the Reformation: a Legacy or a Novelty?" It is exceedingly curious that neither Martin nor Maxwell offer commentary on the order of ecclesiastical discipline. See Martin, pp. 79ff. and Maxwell, pp. 143ff.

[61]*Ibid.*, fo. iiii, r–v, r. The preface was dated 10 February 1559. Within the margins of the text of the preface are summations of the text itself. It appears that they were from a different hand than the author of the preface; it could be argued that the author of the marginal notes thought that the preface was not quite strong enough in its sentiments, and therefore needed amplification.

[62]Davies, p. 39. Cf. Charles David Cremeans, *The Reception of Calvinistic Thought in England* (Urbana: University of Illinois Press, 1949), pp. 117ff.

[63]Cf. Richard T. Hughes and C. Leonard Allen, *Illusions of Innocence. Protestant Primitivism in America, 1630–1875* (Chicago and London: U. of Chicago Press, 1988).

[64]See G. W. Locher, "The Theology of Exile: Faith and the Fate of the Refugee," *Social Groups and Religious Ideas in the Sixteenth Century, Studies in Medieval Culture* (Kalamazoo, 1978) XIII.

[65]Gordon E. Pruett, "A Protestant Doctrine of the Eucharistic Presence," *Calvin Theological Journal* 10 (1975), 142–74. Cf. Peter Norman Brooks, *Thomas Cranmer's Doctrine of the Eucharist* (New York: Macmillan, 1965), and Davies, especially pp. 83ff.

[66]Pruett, "A Protestant Doctrine of the Eucharistic Presence."

[67]See Davies, p. 95. Davies distinguishes between four theories of the eucharistic presence: transubstantiation (Roman Catholic), real presence (Lutheran), virtualism (Calvin, Bucer and Cranmer), and memorialism (Zwingli).

[68]Anthony Gilby, *An Answer to the devilish detection of Stephane Gardiner, Bishoppe of Winchester* (1547), fo. ix, r–lxxiv, r.

[69]Thomas Sampson, *A letter to the trew professors of Christs Gospel...*, fo. Aiii, v–Bii, r.

[70]Davies, p. 106.

[71]*Certen godly, learned, and/ Comfortable conferences...,* in T. H. L. Parker, *English Reformers* (Philadelphia: Westminster Press, 1965), pp. 302ff.

[72]See the annotations on Gen. 4.3, fo. 2, v; Gen. 17.10, fo. 7, r; I Chron. 13.8, fo. 184, v; Ex. 12.11, fo. 29, r.

[73]Annotation on Luke 22.19, fo. 40, v.

[74]Annotation on John 6.62, fo. 46, v.

[75]Locher, "The Theology of Exile: Faith and the Fate of the Refugee," p. 92.

[76]Dan G. Danner, "Christopher Goodman and the English Protestant Tradition of Civil Disobedience," *Sixteenth Century Journal* 8 (1977), 61–73; cf. David H. Wollman, "The Biblical Justification for Resistance to Authority in Ponet's and Goodman's Polemics," *Sixteenth Century Journal* 13 (1982), 29–41; Gerry Bowler, "Marian Protestants and the Idea of Violent Resistance to Tyranny," *Protestantism and the National Church in Sixteenth Century England,* ed. by Peter Lake and Maria Dowling (London: Croom Helm, 1987).

[77]See Danner, "Resistance and the Ungodly Magistrate in the Sixteenth Century: The Marian Exiles," *Journal of the American Academy of Religion* 49 (1981), 471–81.

[78]Richard L. Greaves, "The Nature and Intellectual Milieu of the Political Principles in the Geneva Bible Marginalia," *Journal of Church and State* 22 (1980), 233–49. Greaves seems quite convinced by Robert D. Linder's study of Viret, and postulates that Viret may have been a direct link to the political ideology found in the Geneva Bible. Cf. Robert D. Linder, "Pierre Viret and the Sixteenth Century English Protestants," *Archiv für Reformationsgeschichte* 58 (1967), 149–71. For the background of Continental theories of resistance, see Quentin Skinner, *The Foundations of Modern Political Thought* (Cambridge: University Press 1978), 2 Volumes, especially vol. 2; and, Lowell H. Zuck, ed., *Christianity and Revolution* (Philadelphia: Temple University Press, 1975).

[79]Bowler, "Marian Protestants and the Violent Resistance to Tyranny," p. 140.

[80]Annotations on Gen. 20.9, fo. 8, v; Ex. 34.9, fo. 42, r; Josh. 1.7-8, fo. 97, r; Judg. 17.6, fo. 116, v; 2 Sam. 21.17, fo. 146, r; 2 Kings 12.2, fo. 170, v; Job 34.30, fo. 232, r. Ps. 72.16; fo. 250, r. Cf. Hardin Craig, Jr., "The Geneva Bible as a Political Document," *Pacific Historical Review* 7 (1938), 40–49.

[81]Annotations on Num. 27.21, fo. 75, r; Deut. 17.20, fo. 88, v; 2 Chron. 9.8, fo. 194, v; 2 Chron. 29.3, fo. 202, v. Est. 10.3, fo. 222, r; Ps. 101.6, fo. 256, v.

[82]Fo. 318, v; cf. the annotation on Tit. 3.1, fo. 101, r.

[83]Fo. 122, r.

[84]See Richard L. Greaves, "Calvinism, Democracy, and the Political Thought of John Knox," *Occasional Papers of the American Society for Reformation Research* (1977) I, 81–92.

[85]Richard Bauckham, *Tudor Apocalypse. Sixteenth Century Apocalypticism, Millenarianism and the English Reformation: From John Bale to John Foxe and Thomas Brightman* (Appleford, England: Sutton Courtenay Press, 1978), p. 235.

[86]See Joy Shakespeare, "Plague and Punishment," *Protestantism and the National Church in Sixteenth Century England.*

[87]Cf. Leonard J. Trinterud, "The Origins of Puritanism," *Church History* 20 (1951), 37–57; Trinterud, "A Reappraisal of William Tyndale's Debt to Martin Luther," *Church History* 31 (1962), 24–45; J. G. Møller, "The Beginnings of Puritan Covenant Theology," *Journal of Ecclesiastical History* 14 (1963), 46–67; Richard L. Greaves, "The Origins and Early Development of English Covenant Theology."

[88]Spalding, "Restitution as a Normative Factor for Puritan Dissent." See also J. Wayne Baker, *Heinrich Bullinger and the Covenant: The Other Reformed Tradition* (Athens: Ohio University Press, 1980).

[89]See Bozeman, "Federal Theology and the 'National Covenant': An Elizabethan Presbyterian Case Study." Cf. Michael McGiffert, "God's Controversy with Jacobean England," *American Historical Review* 88 (1983), 1152–53.

[90]Michael McGiffert, "Covenant, Crown, and Commons in Elizabethan Puritanism."

[91]Greaves overstates the influence of Calvin's notion of the covenant on the exiles by failing to recognize its federalist underpinnings; cf. Greaves, "The Origins and Early Development of English Covenant Theology."

[92]Collinson, *Godly People*, p. 22.

[93]See H. C. Porter, *Puritanism in Tudor England*, pp. 55–56.

EPILOGUE

There is an irony to this study as we bring it to conclusion. Many readers would have assumed that the English exiles who spent all or part of the half decade between 1555 and 1560 in Geneva would have become Calvinists. Yet this conclusion does not stand the test of evidence we have witnessed herein. The exiles whose lives and careers we have studied and whose theology we have adumbrated were part of a unique and self-understood English Protestant tradition which does not owe its origin to John Calvin or Geneva. In short, these early English puritans were not Calvinists. Before they arrived in Geneva many of their theological ideas were already in tact, including their doctrine of predestination. Still, it was Calvin and Beza who brought their incipient interest in predestinarian theology to a high pitch during their stay. The one area where the exiles actually borrowed from Geneva was church polity and ecclesiology.

It should be clear, however, that the hermeneutical apparatus was well in place for the exiles to borrow Calvinist ecclesiology. Although it has not been the purpose of the present study to trace the lineage of this English Protestant tradition, Lollardy, Christian humanism and Erasmianism, and the Lutheran influence of Cambridge all could have provided the roots of this uniquely English Reformed tradition. It would not be wise to refer to them as Calvinists, therefore, because they were part of a pan-Protestantism which had humanist ties to Melanchthon, Zwingli, Oecolampadius, Bucer, Capito, and Vadian.[1] It would be later Puritans, even of a more moderate variety and labeled Anglican, who would be more self-consciously Calvinist.[2]

This is not to argue that the English refugee church was not influenced by Calvin and Geneva. It is without doubt that Geneva changed their lives, and many of them used their exile in Geneva as an impetus for clarion calls for radical reform as nonconformists in Elizabethan England. Calvin had a profound effect upon the English church and the theology of its leadership, but it should be clear from what we have seen above that these puritans were not English Calvinists. They were Protestants of the indigenous English Reformed tradition.[3]

While it may be somewhat moot, it is worthwhile to raise the question of who personified the English church at Geneva. Two candidates raise themselves above the others: Whittingham and Gilby (and not John Knox). Whittingham was the genius behind the confession of faith and servicebook, and it was doubtless he who inspired the project of translating the Bible into English. He was perhaps the most competent scholar among the Geneva exiles; his metered psalms rank among the most significant contributions to English Protestantism of the refugee church. Yet he was not the author of enough original material to stand as the one individual who could represent the whole community. It should not be forgotten that he shifted from his former stance with puritan colleagues later in his career by acquiescing to Cecil's pressure to conform in the vestiarian controversy; his cohorts among fellow Geneva exiles viewed his position as a compromise of what they had sternly stood for during and after their exile.

Anthony Gilby, on the other hand, contributed to the literary productions of the church and even may have been the mainstay of the annotations of the 1560 Geneva Bible. His theological interests, as revealed in his original treatises, are closely parallel to the doctrinal emphases characteristic of the annotations of the Geneva Bible. His sacramentarian view of the eucharist was quite in line with the commentary of the marginalia, and his interest in predestination, as evidenced by his early 1553 commentary, is likewise telling. Although there is no tyrannicidal motif in the marginalia, one might conjecture that had Knox, Goodman and Gilby had their way there might have been, for Gilby was not without his radical political views. His Deuteronomic view of history was echoed throughout the marginalia. In fact, Gilby was the paragon of the Geneva brand of puritanism the remainder of his career including a major role in the authorship of the first *Admonition* of 1572. Toward the dusk of his life he was intensely involved in correspondence with a number of principals in the classis movement. The little known name of Anthony Gilby could well be synonymous with the English Protestants who were exiled in Geneva from 1555 to 1560.

A close examination of the theology of the Geneva church invites important theological nuancing along with the conclusion, stated above, that these English Protestants were part of an indigenous English Protestant tradition. Hardly a nuance, the theme which pervades almost everything written by English Protestants during the

Tudor period was England as a covenant nation, the particular bene-
ficiary of God's dramatic activity in history. Their stress on good
works as a natural consequence of God's predestined plan of salvation,
a nuance they inherited from Robert Barnes and William Tyndale,
encouraged the striving for perfection in the child of God; this was a
kind of moralistic understanding of faith which was a departure from
Luther.

The nuance of reading and understanding the Bible was unique to
English Protestantism. When the three marks of the visible church
were adumbrated, it is important to note how the exiles understood
what Luther and Calvin would have emphasized as the proclamation
and hearing of the word of God. The exiles had a narrower view of the
first mark, for it was not simply the proclamation of the true gospel
sola scriptura. Rather it was the Bible itself, as read and understood in
order to find the truth of the gospel of Christ, which they saw as the
mark of the true, visible church. Such a position might even be called
an incipient English Protestant scholasticism. It was surely a biblicism
that characterized few other sixteenth century Protestant traditions.

Ecclesiastical discipline was added as the third mark of the true,
visible church. It is in this context that the exiles' ecclesiology can be
seen in its most dramatic form. The magistrate of God's covenant
nation must lead in the reform of morals as intrinsic to a system of
church government; the exiles refused to place the church under the
state, and the magistrate was subject to the sovereignty of God and in
need of the guidance of the word of God.[4] The state thus had a
churchly function.

The political ideology emerging from the Geneva immigrants was
crucial, and perhaps more than any other issue brought bad light on
the English church and spelled doom for both Knox and Goodman.
Even though the marginalia of the Geneva Bible stop short of any
tyrannicidal polemic, marginal notes accompanying the Old
Testament leave open some possibility of resistance to civil authorities. Whittingham's role in the whole episode still remains curious; his preface to Goodman's book obviously gave it an endorsement. But Whittingham had annotated the 1557 New Testament
without radical political ideas, and most of these notes found their
way into the 1560 edition of the Bible. It is likely that Whittingham
mellowed under the influence of Calvin who was embarrassed by what
Knox and Goodman had written. These radical theories of resistance,
to say nothing of their anti-gynecocratic character, were unique in
the sixteenth century, for they allowed a public overthrow of tyrants
in the event lesser magistrates failed to act.

We have seen that predestination was an important doctrine for the Geneva church. Their view was oriented toward a doctrine of God to ensure divine transcendence and sovereignty rather than as intrinsic to salvation. The double-decree motif was standard for the exiles, and it appeared in a mature rather than an evolved form. Knox seemed closer to Calvin, Gilby closer to Beza. There is no evidence to suggest, however, that Gilby borrowed his predestinarian theology from Geneva; his own views antedated Beza's writings on the subject.

The exiles' biblical hermeneutic was a primitivist paradigm: they looked to scripture for a pattern or model which could be restituted or duplicated in their own times. This would lead them to a rather restrictive biblicism which was different from either Luther or Calvin, although close to Zwingli's position, and ironically closer yet to Anabaptist hermeneutics.

The eucharistic theology of the exiles was certainly more closely aligned with Zurich than the Reformed tradition represented by Bucer, Calvin, Peter Martyr and even Thomas Cranmer. The distinction between a sign and what it signified, the eating and drinking of Christ's body only spiritually and not carnally for the refreshment of the soul, and the lack of emphasis on partaking by faith, all characteristic of Gilby's polemic and the marginalia of the Geneva Bible, were clearly sacramentarian in emphasis and character.

Perhaps above all, this study has drawn attention yet again to the importance of the Geneva Bible of 1560. Its popularity in Elizabethan England was remarkable, and in the early decades of the seventeenth century even the Authorized Version could not supplant its popularity and influence; some of the first editions of the King James Version were printed with the marginalia of the Geneva Bible. The annotations and marginal paraphernalia were the chief legacy of the Geneva Bible, for in them was contained a definite theological labyrinth which became an integral part of the sacred text.

The puritans we have met were indeed people of the book. It may sound truistic to portray any Protestant tradition this way, but the English Protestant attachment to the Bible was *sui generis*. The Bible was the source for their theology, church order and piety, even their national collective consciousness. When they returned to the original sources of Christian antiquity and the model set by the Lord's apostles, they felt themselves on the surest of foundations.

NOTES

[1]See Yost, "A Reappraisal of How Protestantism Spread during the Early English Reformation," who inverts the influence question to suggest it was humanists who were influenced by a process of Protestantization and thus took an active role in the Reformation. Cf. C. M. Dent, *Protestant Reformers in Elizabethan Oxford* (Oxford: University Press, 1983).

[2]See VanderMolen, "Anglican Against Puritan: Ideological Origins During the Marian Exile," and Peter Lake, "Calvinism and the English Church," *Past and Present* 114 (1987), 32–76.

[3]Cremeans, *The Reception of Calvinistic Thought in England,* pp. 25f.

[4]See Davies, *Worship and Theology in England from Cranmer to Hooker, 1534–1603*, p. 61.

BIBLIOGRAPHY

A Brief declaration of the chiefe poyntes of Christian Religion, set forth in a Table (Geneva: Printed by Jo. Rivery, 1556).

*A brief and pithie Summe of Christian faithe made in the forme of a confession...*Made by Theod. De Beza. Translated out of French by R.F. (London, 1589).

A Brieff Discours off the Troubles Begonne at Franckford, 1554–1558 A.D. (London: Elliot Stock, 1575).

A Check or reproofe of M. Howlets vntimely shreeching in her maiesties eares, with an answer to the reasons alleadged in a discourse thereunto annexed, why Catholickes...refuse to goe to church... (London, 1581).

A Commentarye upon the Epistle of Saint Paul to the Romans, written in Latine by M. Iohn Caluin, and newly translated into Englishe by Christopher Rosdell (London: 1583).

A Faithfvl and Most Godly treatyse concerning the most sacred sacrament of the blessed body and bloud of our Sauior Christ, ts. by Miles Coverdale (London: John Day, 1550).

A notable and comfortable exposition, vpon the fovrth of Mathew, concerning the tentations of Christ, Preached in S. Peters Church, Oxenford. Thomas Bentham, London (n.d.).

A Treatise on the right way from Danger of Sinne & vengeance in this wicked world, vnto godly wealth and saluation in christe. Made by Th. Leuer, and now newly augmented. Printed by Henrie Bynneman for George Byshop (London, 1575).

A treatise conteining certain meditations of trew and perfect consolation (London, n.d.)

An Admonition to Parliament (London, 1572).

Archbold, W.A.J. *Dictionary of National Biography*, ed. Leslie Stephen (New York: Macmillan, 1908) (hereafter cited *DNB*), XVII, 946–47.

Baker, J. Wayne. *Heinrich Bullinger and the Covenant: The Other Reformed Tradition* (Athens: Ohio University Press, 1980).

Bale, John. *Scriptorum illustrium maioris Brytanniae...* (Basel, 1557–59).

Bartlett, Kenneth R. "The Role of the Marian Exiles," in P. W. Hasler, *The House of Commons 1558–1603* (London: The History of Parliament Trust, 1981), I, 102–10.

Bauckham, Richard. "Marian Exiles and Cambridge Puritanism: James Pilkington's 'Halfe a Score'," *Journal of Ecclesiastical History* 26 (1975), 137–48.

_____. *Tudor Apocalypse. Sixteenth Century Apocalypticism, Millenarianism and the English Reformation: From John Bale to John Foxe and Thomas Brightman* (Appleford, England: Sutton Courtenay Press, 1978).

Bayne, Ronald. *DNB*, VI, 1304.

Betteridge, Maurice S. "The Bitter Notes: The Geneva Bible and Its Annotations," *Sixteenth Century Journal* 14 (1983), 41–62.

Bindoff, S. T. *Tudor England* (London: Penguin, 1964).

Bloxam, John Rouse. *A Register of the Presidents, Fellows, Demies...of Saint Mary Magdalen College* (Oxford: W. Graham, 1853).

Bowker, Margaret. *The Secular Clergy in the Diocese of Lincoln, 1495–1520* (Cambridge: University Press, 1969).

Bowler, Gerry "Marian Protestants and the Idea of Violent Resistance to Tyranny," *Protestantism and the National Church in Sixteenth Century England*, ed. by Peter Lake and Maria Dowling (London: Croom Helm, 1987).

Bozeman, Theodore Dwight. "Federal Theology and the 'National Covenant': An Elizabethan Presbyterian Case Study," *Church History* 61 (1992), 394–407.

Bradley, E. T. *DNB*, VII, 1218–19.

_____. *DNB*, VIII, 128–30.

Bray, John S. *Theodore Beza's Doctrine of Predestination* (Nieuwkoop: B. DeGraaf, 1975).

Brigen, Susan. *London and the Reformation* (Oxford: University Press, 1989).

Brit. Mus. Harle. Ms. l, 416.31.

Brit. Mus. Lansd. Ms. 982.78.

British Mus. Add. Ms. 32091.

Brook, Benjamin. *The Lives of the Puritans* (London: James Black, 1813).

Brooks, Peter Norman. *Thomas Cranmer's Doctrine of the Eucharist* (New York: Macmillan, 1965).

Burn, J. Southerden. *History of Parish Registers* in Laing, *Works of John Knox* (New York: AMS, 1966).

Calendar of the State Papers, Domestic, 1547–80, ed. by Robert Lemon (London: Longman, Brown et. al., 1856).

Calvin, John. *Institutes of the Christian Religion,* ts. and annot. by Ford Lewis Battles (Grand Rapids: Eerdmans, 1975).

Cambridge University Library Mss., Ely Add. 49.

Cambridge University Library, Baker Mss., Vol. 31, Mm. 1.42.

Cambridge University Library, Baker Mss., Vol. 31, Mm. 1.43.

Cambridge University Library, Baker Mss., Vol. 32, Mm. 1.43.

Cambridge University Library, Ms. Hib. 5.55.1.

Carlyle, E. Irving. *DNB*, XXI, 175.

Certen godly, learned, and/ Comfortable conferences... in T. H. L. Parker, *English Reformers* (Philadelphia: Westminster Press, 1965).

Cherry, Althea Vadrienne. "The Life and Political Theories of Christopher Goodman," (M.A. Dissertation, University of Chicago, 1935).

Christenson, Paul. "Reformers and the Church of England under Elizabeth I and the Early Stuarts," *Journal of Ecclesiastical History* 31 (1980), 463–87.

Clancy, S.J., Thomas. "Papist-Protestant-Puritan: English Religious Taxonomy 1565–1665," *Recusant History* 13 (1976), 227–53.

Clark, Peter. *English Provincial Society from the Reformation to the Revolution. Religion, Politics and Society in Kent, 1500–1640* (Hassocks, Sussex: Harvester, 1977).

Clebsch, William A. *England's Earliest Protestants 1520–1535* (New Haven: Yale University Press, 1964).

Cole, William. *Warhafftige zeitung Bom auffgang des Evangelii...* (Geneva, 1559).

Colligan, J. Hay. *The Honourable William Whittingham of Chester* (London: Simpkin Marshall, 1934).

Collinson, Patrick. "A Comment: Concerning the Name Puritan," *Journal of Ecclesiastical History,* 31 (1980) 488.

_____. "Role of Women in the English Reformation Illustrated by the Life and Friendships of Anne Locke," *Studies in Church History*, ed. G. J. Cuming (London: Thomas Nelson and Sons, 1965).

_____. "The Elizabethan Church and the New Religion," *The Reign of Elizabeth I* (Athens: University of Georgia Press, 1985).

_____. *Elizabethan Puritan Movement* (Berkeley: University of California Press, 1967).

_____. "The Authorship of *A Brieff Discours off the Troubles Begonne at Franckford,*" *Journal of Ecclesiastical History* 9 (1958), 188–209.

_____. *Godly People. Essays on English Protestantism and Puritanism* (London: Hambledon Press, 1983).

Commentaries of that diuine Iohn Caluine, vpon the Prophet Daniell... (London: John Day, 1570).

Coolidge, John S. *The Pauline Renaissance in England. Puritanism and the Bible* (London: Clarendon Press, 1970).

Cooper, C. H. and Thompson Cooper, *Athenae Cantabrigienses* (Cambridge: Deighton, et.al., 1861).

Cooper, Thompson. *DNB*, L, 232–33.

Coverdale, Miles. *Certain most godly, fruitful, and comfortable letters of such true Saints and holy Martyrs of God* (London: John Day, 1564).

Cowell, Henry J. "The Sixteenth-century English-speaking Refugee Churches at Geneva and Frankfort," *Proceedings of the Huguenot Society of Great Britain and Ireland* 16 (1939), 209–30.

Craig, Jr. Hardin. "The Geneva Bible as a Political Document," *Pacific Historical Review* 7 (1938), 40–49.

Cranmer, Thomas. *Homily of Salvation* in *Miscellaneous Writings and Letters of Thomas Cranmer*, ed. for the Parker Society by John Edmund Cox (Cambridge: University Press, 1846).

Cremeans, Charles David. *The Reception of Calvinistic Thought in England* (Urbana: University of Illinois Press, 1949).

Cross, Clare. *Church and People 1450–1660* (London: Fontana, 1976).

Danner, Dan G. "Christopher Goodman and the English Protestant Tradition of Civil Disobedience," *Sixteenth Century Journal* 8 (1977), 61–73.

_____. "Anthony Gilby: Puritan in Exile—A Biographical Approach," *Church History* 40 (1971), 412–22.

_____. "Calvin and Puritanism: The Career of William Whittingham," *Calviniana. Ideas and Influence of Jean Calvin*, Robert V. Schnucker ed., *Sixteenth Century Essays & Studies* (1988), X, 151–63.

_____. "Resistance and the Ungodly Magistrate in the Sixteenth Century: The Marian Exiles," *Journal of the American Academy of Religion* 49 (1981), 471–81.

_____. "The Contribution of the Geneva Bible of 1560 to the English Protestant Tradition," *Sixteenth Century Journal* 12 (1981), 5–18.

Davies, Horton. *Worship and Theology in England from Cranmer to Hooker, 1534–1603* (Princeton: Princeton University Press, 1970).

Davies, J. F. *Heresy and Reformation in the South-East of England 1520–1559* (London: Royal Historical Society, 1983).

Denis, Philippe. "'Discipline' in the English Huguenot Churches of the Reformation: A Legacy or a Novelty?" *Proceedings of the Huguenot Society of London* 23 (1979), 166–71.

Dickens, A. G. and Dorothy Carr. *The Reformation in England to the Accession of Elizabeth I* (London: Arnold, 1967).

Dickens, A. G. *The English Reformation* (London: Collins, 1964), rev. Second Edition (University Park, Pennsylvania: Pennsylvania State University Press, 1989).

Dowson, Jane E. A. "The Early Career of Christopher Goodman and His Place in the Development of English Protestant Thought" (Ph.D. Dissertation, University of Durham, 1978).

Elton, G. R. *England under the Tudors* (London: Methuen, 1955).

English Reprints. Sermons of Thomas Lever, ed. Edward Arber (London: 1870), V.xii.

Foster, Joseph. *Alumni Oxonienses* (Oxford: J. Parker & Co., 1891).

Fowler, Thomas. *History of Corpus Christi College with Lists of its Members* (Oxford: Oxford Historical Society, 1893).

Foxe, John. *Acts and Monuments*, ed. Stephen R. Cattley (London: Seeley and Burside, 1837).

Gardiner, Stephen. *A Detection of the Devil's Sophistrie, wherewith he robbeth the unlearned people of the true belief, in the most blessed Sacrament of the aulter* (no colophon, 1546).

Garrett, Christina H. *The Marian Exiles. A Study in the Origins of Elizabethan Puritanism* (Cambridge: University Press, 1938).

Gilby, Anthony. *A Briefe Treatise of Election and Reprobation, with certen answers to the obiections of the aduersaries of thys doctrine* (Geneva, 1556).

_____. *Tracts Concerning Vestments* (no colophon or date).

_____. *View of Antichrist* in *A Part of a register...* (no colophon or date).

_____. *A Commentarye upon the Prophet Mycah* (London, 1551).

_____. *A Pleasavnt Dialogve, Betweene a Souldior of Barwicke, and an English Chaplaine...* (no colophon, 1581).

_____. *An Answer to the devilish detection of Stephane Gardiner, Bishoppe of Winchester* (no colophon, 1547).

Godly prayers and Meditations, paraphrasticallye made upon all the Psalms... translated out of the French into Englishe (London, 1577).

Goodman, Christopher. *How Svperior Powers Oght to be Obeyd...* (Geneva, 1558).

Goodwin, Alfred. *DNB*, II, 68–69.

Greaves, Richard L. "Calvinism, Democracy, and the Political Thought of John Knox," *Occasional Papers of the American Society for Reformation Research* (1977), I, 81-92.

_____. "John Knox and the Covenant Tradition," *Journal of Ecclesiastical History* 24 (1973), 23–32.

_____. "The Nature and Intellectual Milieu of the Political Principles in the Geneva Bible Marginalia," *Journal of Church and State* 22 (1980), 233–49.

_____. *Theology and Revolution in the Scottish Reformation: Studies in the Thought of John Knox* (Grand Rapids: Christian University Press, 1980).

_____. "The Origins and Early Development of English Covenant Thought," *The Historian* 31 (1968), 21–35.

Green, Mary Anne Everett., ed. *Life and Death of Mr. William Whittingham, from a ms. in Anthony Wood's Collection*, Bodlein Library, Oxford (printed for the Camden Society, 1870).

Grosart, A. B. *DNB*, II, 284.

Hackett, Horatio B. "Church-Book of the Puritans at Geneva, from 1555 to 1560," *Bibliotheca Sacra* (1892) 469.

Hadden, J. Cathbert. *DNB*, XI, 73–74.

Haigh, Christopher. "Some Aspects of the Recent Historiography of the English Reformation," *Stadtbürgertum und Adel in der Reformation: Studien zur*

Sozialgeschichte der Reformation in England und Deutschland, ed. by Wolfgang J. Mommsen (Stuttgard: Klett-Cotta, 1979).

_____. *Reformation and Resistance in Tudor Lancashire* (Cambridge: University Press, 1975).

_____. "The Church of England, the Catholics and the People," *The Reign of Elizabeth I* (Athens: University of Georgia Press, 1985).

_____. *The English Reformation Revised* (Cambridge: University Press, 1987).

Hall, Basil. "Puritanism: the Problem of Definition," *Studies in Church History* (1965), II, 283–96.

Hargrave, O. T. "The Predestinarian Offensive of the Marian Exiles at Geneva," *Historical Magazine of the Protestant Episcopal Church* 42 (1973), 111–23.

Haugaard, W. P. "The Episcopal Pretentions of Thomas Sampson," *Historical Magazine of the Protestant Episcopal Church* 36 (1967), 383–86.

Haugaard, William A. *Elizabeth and the English Reformation* (Cambridge: University Press, 1968).

Heyer, Th. "Notice sur la Colonie Anglais, Ètablie à Genève de 1555 à 1560," *Memoires et Documents, publiés par la Sociétié d'archéologie de Genèva* IX (1855), 337–68.

Hughes, Philip E. *The Reformation in England,* Rev. Ed. (London: Burns and Oates, 1963).

_____. *Theology of the English Reformers* (London: Hodder and Stoughton, 1965).

Hughes, Richard T. and C. Leonard Allen. *Illusions of Innocence. Protestant Primitivism in America, 1630–1875* (Chicago and London: U. of Chicago Press, 1988).

Hurstfield, Joel, ed. *The Reformation Crisis* (London: Arnold, 1965).

Ioannis Calvini Opera, ed. G. Baum, et. al. (M. Bruhn, 1876).

James, Mervyn. *Family, Lineage and Civil Society: A Study of Society, Politics and Mentality in the Durham Region, 1500–1640* (Oxford: Clarendon Press, 1974).

Jones, Norman L. *Faith by Statute. Parliament and the Settlement of Religion, 1559* (London: Royal Historical Society, 1982).

Kendall, R. T. *Calvin and English Calvinism to 1649* (New York: Oxford University Press, 1979).

Kethe, William. *A Sermon made at Blanford Forum, in the countie of Dorset on Wensday the 17. of Ianury last past at the session holden there, before the honoble and worshippefull of that Shyre...* (London: John Day, 1571).

_____. *Unto the ryghte honorable the nobilitie and ientlemen of England* (no colophon or date).

Knox, John. *First Blast of the Trumpet against the Monstrovs Regiment of Women* (Geneva, 1558).

_____. *History of the Reformation in Scotland* in Laing, *Works of John Knox* (Edinburgh: James Thin, 1895).

Knox, Samuel James. *John Knox's Genevan Congregation* (The Presbyterian Historical Society of England, 1956).

_____. "Christopher Goodman—A Forgotten Presbyterian," *Journal of the Presbyterian Historical Society* 28 (1950), 221–32.

_____. "A Study of the Genevan Exiles and their Influence upon the Rise of Nonconformity in England" (M.A. Thesis, Trinity College, Dublin, 1953).

Laing, David. *Works of John Knox* (Edinburgh: James Thin, 1895).

Lake, Peter D. *Anglicans and Puritans? Presbyterianism and English Conformist Thought from Whitgift to Hooker* (London: Unwin Hyman, 1988).

_____. "Calvinism and the English Church," *Past and Present* 114 (1987) 32-76.

Lee, Sidney. *DNB*, XI, 1021–22.

Letters of Thomas Wood, ed. Patrick Collinson (London: University/Athone Press, 1960).

Linder, Robert D. "Pierre Viret and the Sixteenth Century English Protestants," *Archiv für Reformationsgeschichte* 58 (1967), 149–71.

156   *Bibliography*

Locher, G. W. "The Theology of Exile: Faith and the Fate of the Refugee," *Social Groups and Religious Ideas in the Sixteenth Century, Studies in Medieval Culture* (Kalamazoo, 1978), XIII.

_____. "Zwinglis Einflus in England und Schottland—Daten und Probleme," *Zwingliana* 14 (1975), 165–209.

Lorimer, Peter. *John Knox and the Church of England* (London: H. S. King, 1875).

MacKay, Aeneas. *DNB*, XI, 308–28.

Maitland, S. R. *Essays on Subjects Connected with the Reformation in England* (London: J. Lane, 1899).

Martin, Charles. *Les Protestants Anglais réfugiés à Genève au temps de Calvin 1555–1560* (Geneva: A. Jullian, 1915).

Maxwell, W. D. *John Knox's Genevan Service Book, 1556* (Edinburgh: Oliver and Boyd, 1931).

McGiffert, Michael. "Covenant, Crown, and Commons in Elizabethan Puritanism," *Journal of British Studies* 20 (1980), 32–52.

_____. "William Tyndale's Conception of Covenant," *Journal of Ecclesiastical History* 32 (1981), 167–84.

_____. "God's Controversy with Jacobean England," *American Historical Review* 88 (1983), 1152–53.

McLelland, Joseph C. *The Visible Words of God* (Grand Rapids: Wm. B. Eerdmans, 1957).

Mitchell, A. F. ed. *Livre des Anglois or Register of the English Church at Geneva under the Pastoral Care of Knox and Goodman 1555–1559* (no colophon or date).

Møller, J. G. "The Beginnings of Puritan Covenant Theology," *Journal of Ecclesiastical History* 14 (1963), 46–67.

Mozley, J. F. *Coverdale and His Bibles* (London: Lutterworth Press, 1953).

N. D. [Robert Parsons]. *The Third Part of a Treatise Intitled: of three Conversions of England: conteyninge...The First Six Months* (1604).

Neale, J. E. "The Elizabethan Acts of Supremacy and Uniformity," *English Historical Review* 65 (1950), 304–32.

Norwood, Frederick A. "The Marian Exiles—Denizens or Sojourners? *Church History* 13 (1944), 100–10.

_____. "The Strangers' 'Model Churches' in Sixteenth Century England," *Reformation Studies. Essays in Honor of Roland H. Bainton* (Richmond: John Knox Press, 1962).

O'Day, Rosemary. *The Debate on the English Reformation* (London and New York: Methuen, 1986).

_____. "Thomas Bentham: A Case Study in the Problems of the Early Elizabethan Episcopate," *Journal of Ecclesiastical History* 23 (1972), 137–59.

Original Letters Relative to the English Reformation...from the Archives of Zurich, ed. for the Parker Society by Hastings Robinson (Cambridge: University Press, 1846).

Parte of a register, contayninge sundrie matters, written by diuers godly and learned in our time, which stand for, and desire the reformation of our church, in Discipline and ceremonies, according to the pure worde of God, and the Lawe of our Lande (London, 1593).

Peel, Albert. "A Sermon of Christopher Goodman's in 1583," *Journal of the Presbyterian Historical Society of England* 9 (1949), 80–93.

Pettegree, Andrew. "Re-Writing the English Reformation," *Nederlands Archief voor Kerkgeschiedenis* (1992), 37–58.

_____. *Marian Protestantism: Six Studies* (Hampshire, England: Scolar Press, 1996).

Philips, Walter. "Henry Bullinger and the Elizabethan Vestiarian Controversy: An Analysis of Influence," *Journal of Religious History* 11 (1981), 363–84.

Pollard A . W. and G. R. Redgrave, *A Short Title Catalogue of Books Printed in England, Scotland and Ireland ...1475–1640* (London: Bernard Quaritch Ltd., 1926).

Pollard, A. F. *Henry VIII* (New York: Harper Torchbooks, 1966).

_____. *DNB,* LXI, 150-53.

_____. *Records of the English Bible, the Documents Relating to the Translation and Publication of the Bible in English, 1525–1611* (London: Oxford University Press, 1911).

_____. *Thomas Cranmer and the English Reformation, 1489–1556* (London: Frank Cass, 1965).

_____. *Wolsey: Church and State in Sixteenth Century England* (New York: Harper Torchbooks, 1966).

Porter, H. C. *Puritanism in Tudor England* (London: Macmillan, 1970).

Primus, J. H. *The Vestments Controversy: An Historical Study of the Earliest Tensions Within the Church of England in the Reign of Edward VI and Elizabeth* (N. V. Hampton, 1960).

Pruett, Gordon E. "A Protestant Doctrine of the Eucharistic Presence," *Calvin Theological Journal* 10 (1975), 142–74.

Psalms of Dauid Trvly Opened and explaned by Paraphrasis... (Henry Denham, 1581).

Read, Conyers. *Bibliography of British History: Tudor Period, 1485–1603* (Oxford: Clarendon Press 1933).

Reid, W. Stanford. *Trumpeter of God: A Biography of John Knox* (New York: Charles Scribner's Sons, 1974).

Remains of Myles Coverdale, ed. for the Parker Society by George Pearson (Cambridge: University Press, 1846).

Ridley, Jasper. *John Knox* (Oxford: Clarendon Press, 1968).

Ridley, Nicholas. *Certen godly, learned, and/ comfortable conferences, betwene the two Reuerende Fathers, and holye martyrs of/Christ, D. Nicolas Rydley late Bysshoppe of London, and M. Hughe Latymer/ Sometyme Bysshoppe of Wor-/cester, during the time of theyr empryson-/ments. Whereunto is added./ A Treatise agayst the error of Transubstan-/tiation, made by the sayd Reuerende Father D./ Nicolas Rydley./ M.D.LVI* (no colophon).

Sampson, Thomas. *A letter to the trew professors of Christs Gospel/ inhabitinge in the Parish off Allhallowis/ in Bredstrete in London* (Strasburg 1554).

_____. *A Warning to take heede of Fowlers Psalter* (imprinted at London by Thomas Vautrollier for George Bishop, 1578).

_____. *A Briefe collection of the Church, and of certayne ceremonies thereof* (London: H. Middleton, 1581).

Sarcerius, Erasmus. *Common places of scripture orderly...set forth...to the great profyte and help of all such studentes in gods worde...* translated into English by Richard Taverner (no colophon, 1538).

Scarisbrick, J. J. *Henry VIII* (London: Eyre and Spottiswoode, 1968).

_____. *The Reformation and the English People* (Oxford: Blackwell, 1984).

Select Poetry. Ed. for the Parker Society by Edward Farr (Cambridge: University Press, 1845).

Shakespeare, Joy. "Plague and Punishment," *Protestantism and the National Church in Sixteenth Century England,* ed. by Peter Lake and Maria Dowling (London: Croom Helm, 1987).

Shaw, W. A. *DNB*, XVI, 460.

Skinner, Quentin. *The Foundations of Modern Political Thought* (Cambridge: University Press 1978).

Southgate, W. M. "The Marian Exiles and the Influence of John Calvin," *History* 27 (1942), 148–52.

Spalding, James C. "Restitution as a Normative Factor for Puritan Dissent, *Journal of the American Academy of Religion* 44 (1976), 47–63.

_____. "The *Reformatio Legum Ecclesiasticarum* of 1552 and the Furthering of Discipline in England," *Church History* 39 (1970), 162–71.

Strype, John. *Annals of the Reformation* (Oxford: Clarendon Press, 1824).

_____. *Ecclesiastical Memorials* (Oxford: Clarendon Press, 1822).

_____. *The Life and Acts of Edmund Grindal* (Oxford: Clarendon Press, 1821).

_____. *The Life and Acts of Matthew Parker* (Oxford: Clarendon Press, 1821).

Sutherland, N. M. "The Marian Exiles and the Establishment of the Elizabethan Regime," *Archiv für Reformationsgeschichte* 78 (1987), 253–84.

Tedder, H. R. *DNB*, IV, 1289–97.

The forme of prayers and Ministration of the Sacraments, &c, vsed in the Englishe Congregation at Geneua: and approued, by the famous and godly learned man, Iohn Caluyn (Imprinted at Geneva by Iohn Crespin, 1556).

The Geneva Bible: A Facsimile of the 1560 Edition, ed. L. E. Berry (Madison: University of Wisconsin Press, 1969).

The Second Part of a Register, ed. Albert Peel (Cambridge: University Press, 1915).

Tractatus de praedestinatione. Works of James Pilkington, Bishop of Durham, ed. for the Parker Society by James Scholefield (Cambridge: University Press, 1842).

Trinterud, Leonard J. "The Origins of Puritanism," *Church History* 20 (1951), 37–57.

_____. "A Reappraisal of William Tyndale's Debt to Martin Luther," *Church History* 31 (1962), 24–45.

Two bokes of the noble doctor and B.S. Augustine theone entitled of the Predestination of saints, thother of perserueraunce vnto thende..., translated out of Laten into Englishe by John Scory the late B. of Chichester, 1555 (10 Calen. Martij).

Two Notable Sermons, Made by that worthy Martyr of Christ, Master Iohn Bradford: the one of Repentance, and the other of the Lords Supper, now newly imprinted, ts. by Thomas Sampson (London, 1599).

Tyndale, William. *The Prophet Jonas with an introduccion before teachinge to understand him* (Antwerp, 1531?).

_____. *Five Books of Moses called the Pentateuch, being a verbatim reprint of the edition of 1530* (Carbondale: Southern Illinois University Press, 1967).

VanderMolen, Ronald J. "Anglican Against Puritan: Ideological Origins During the Marian Exile," *Church History* 42 (1973), 45–57.

_____. "Providence as Mystery, Providence as Revelation: Puritan and Anglican Modifications of John Calvin's Doctrine of Providence," *Church History* 47 (1978), 27–47.

Venables, Canon. *DNB*, IV, 730–32.

Venn, John and J. A. Venn. *Alumni catabrigienses* (Cambridge: University Press, 1922).

Verkamp, Bernard J. "The Zwinglians and Adiaphorism," *Church History* 42 (1973), 486–504.

_____. *The Indifferent Mean: Adiaphorism in the English Reformation to 1554* (Athens: Ohio University Press, 1977).

Wallace, Dewey D. "The Doctrine of Predestination in the Early English Reformation," *Church History* 43 (1974), 201–15.

_____. *Puritans and Predestination: Grace in English Protestant Theology* (Chapel Hill: University of North Carolina Press, 1982).

Wendel, François. *Calvin: The Origin and Development of His Religious Thought,* ts. Philip Mairet (London: Wm. Collins, 1963).

White, Peter. *Predestination, Policy and Polemic. Conflict and Consensus in the English Church from the Reformation to the Civil War* (Cambridge: University Press, 1992).

Whittingham, William. *To My faythfull Brethren now afflyted, and to all those that unfaynedly loue the Lorde Jesus...* (no colophon, 1566?).

Wollman, David H. "The Biblical Justification for Resistance to Authority in Ponet's and Goodman's Polemics," *Sixteenth Century Journal* 13 (1982) 29–41.

Wood, Anthony. *Athenae Oxonienses*, Bliss ed. (Hildesheim: Georg Olms, 1969).

Writings and Translations of Myles Coverdale, ed. for the Parker Society by George Pearson (Cambridge: University Press, 1844).

Yost, John K. "A Reappraisal of How Protestantism Spread during the Early English Reformation," *Anglican Theological Journal* 60 (1978), 437–46.

Zuck, Lowell H., ed. *Christianity and Revolution* (Philadelphia: Temple University Press, 1975).

INDEX

Index

Studies in Church History

General Editor: William L. Fox

This series in Church history offers a place for diverse scholarship that is sometimes too particularly calibrated for any other publishing category. Rather, the richness of the Church history series is in its scope, which variously mixes historical theology and historical hermeneutics, doctrine and practices of piety, religious or spiritual movements, and institutional configurations. Western Europe and the United States continue to provide grounds for exploration and discourse, but this series will also publish books on Christianity in Asia, Africa, and Latin America. Traditional periodization (Early Christian, Medieval, Reformation and Modern eras) grants maximum representation.

The particular focus of the series is the treatment of religious thought as being vital to the historical context and outcome of Christian experience. Fresh interpretations of classic and well-known Christian thinkers (e.g., Augustine, Luther, Calvin, Edwards, etc.) using multicultural perspectives, the critical approaches of feminist and men's studies form the foundation of the series. Meanwhile, new voices from Christian history need illumination and explication by church historians in this series. Authors who are versatile enough to "cross-over" disciplinary boundaries have enormous opportunity in this series to reach an international audience.

For additional information about this series or for the submission of manuscripts, please contact:

Peter Lang Publishing
Acquistions Dept.
516 N. Charles St., 2nd Floor
Baltimore, MD 21201

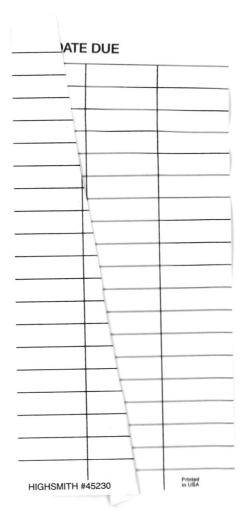

DATE DUE